THE LEGEND OF
KYRANDIA™

THE OFFICIAL STRATEGY GUIDE

SECRETS OF THE GAMES
NOW AVAILABLE FROM PRIMA

Computer Game Books

The 7th Guest: The Official Strategy Guide
Aces Over Europe: The Official Strategy Guide
Alone in the Dark: The Official Strategy Guide
Betrayal at Krondor: The Official Strategy Guide
CD-ROM Games Secrets, Volume 1
Computer Adventure Games Secrets
DOOM Battlebook
DOOM II: The Official Strategy Guide
Dracula Unleashed: The Official Strategy Guide & Novel
Harpoon II: The Official Strategy Guide
Lemmings: The Official Companion (with disk)
Master of Orion: The Official Strategy Guide
Microsoft Flight Simulator: The Official Strategy Guide
Microsoft Space Simulator: The Official Strategy Guide
Might and Magic Compendium: The Authorized Strategy Guide for Games I, II, III, and IV
Myst: The Official Strategy Guide
Outpost: The Official Strategy Guide
Pagan: Ultima VIII—The Ultimate Strategy Guide
Prince of Persia: The Official Strategy Guide
Quest for Glory: The Authorized Strategy Guide
Rebel Assault: The Official Insider's Guide
Return to Zork Adventurer's Guide
Shadow of the Comet: The Official Strategy Guide
Sherlock Holmes, Consulting Detective: The Unauthorized Strategy Guide
Sid Meier's Civilization, or Rome on 640K a Day
SimCity 2000: Power, Politics, and Planning
SimEarth: The Official Strategy Guide
SimFarm Almanac: The Official Guide to SimFarm
SimLife: The Official Strategy Guide
SSN-21 Seawolf: The Official Strategy Guide
Strike Commander: The Official Strategy Guide and Flight School
Stunt Island: The Official Strategy Guide
SubWar 2050: The Official Strategy Guide (with disk)
TIE Fighter: The Official Strategy Guide
Ultima: The Avatar Adventures
Ultima VII and Underworld: More Avatar Adventures
Wing Commander I and II: The Ultimate Strategy Guide
X-Wing: The Official Strategy Guide

How to Order:

For information on quantity discounts contact the publisher: Prima Publishing, P.O. Box 1260BK, Rocklin, CA 95677-1260; (916) 632-4400. On your letterhead include information concerning the intended use of the books and the number of books you wish to purchase. For individual orders, turn to the back of the book for more information.

THE LEGEND OF
KYRANDIA ™

THE OFFICIAL STRATEGY GUIDE

Joe Hutsko

PRIMA PUBLISHING
P.O. Box 1260 BK
Rocklin, CA 95677-1260

Publisher, Entertainment: Roger Stewart
Managing Editor: Paula Munier Lee
Senior Acquisitions Editor: Hartley G. Lesser
Acquisitions Editor: Ed Dille
Creative Director, Secrets of the Games: Rusel DeMaria
Project Editor: Brett Skogen
Cover Production Coordinator: Anne Flemke
Copy Editor: Kelley Mitchell
Technical Reviewer: Rick Gush
Book Design and Layout: Peter Hancik, Eurodesign
Cover Illustration: Rick Parks
Adaptations to Cover: Page Design, Inc.

ISBN: 1-55958-782-2

Library of Congress Catalog Card Number: 94-69168

Printed in the United States of America

95 96 97 98 CWO 10 9 8 7 6 5 4 3 2 1

CONTENTS

Acknowledgments . . . . *xii*
Preface . . . . *xiii*

✦ BOOK I ✦
THE LEGEND OF KYRANDIA I

1 Grampa's Bad Hair Day **3**
Brandon's Homeland 4
The Weary Willow 5
Brynn's Temple 5
Pool of Sorrow 7
Forest Altar 7
Herman and the Ruined Bridge 9
Return to Brynn's Temple 10
Crossing the Bridge 10

2 Timbermist Woods and Darm **13**
The Wizard Darm 14
Old Nolby and The Oldest Oak Tree 15

Songbird's Nest 16
The Bubbling Spring 16
Deadwood Glade 16
The Yellow Amulet Gem 17
The Birthstone Quest 18
The Marble Altar 19
The Ruby Tree 21
Serpent's Grotto 21
Say Good-bye to Darm 22

3 **Shadowrealm Labyrinth** **27**
Natural Mineral Pool 28
Why Am I Here, Anyway? (Or, The Iron Gate) 29
Fireberry Bushes 29
The Chasm of Everfall 30
The Pantheon of Moonlight 31
The Cavern of Twilight 32
The Emerald Cave 32
Unlocking the Gate 34
Back to Shadowrealm 34
The Purple Amulet Gem 35
Volcanic River 35
Crossing to Safety (Sort of) 37

4 **Faeriewood and Zanthia** **41**
Knocking Some Sense 42
Zanthia's Lab 43
The Fountain and Malcolm 44
The Burning Tree 46
Back to Zanthia with the Magic Water 46
The Other Side of Faeriewood 47
Bubble, Bubble, Toil and Troublesome Potions 49
Making New Potions 50
The Royal Chalice 51
A Natural Clearing and Faun's Home 52
Leaving Faeriewood 53

5 **Castle Kyrandia and The Big Showdown** **59**
A Misty Grave (Mama Mia) 60
The Castle Gate 61

Malcolm Revisited 61
The Great Hall 63
The Kitchen 64
The Library 64
The Catacombs 65
Upstairs 65
The Royal Foyer 66
Malcolm! 66
The Kyra-Vault 67
Kyrandia Is Saved! 67

✤ BOOK 2 ✤
THE HAND OF FATE   75

6 Darkmoor Swamp **77**
The Tossed Lab 78
Get The Gear 78
Ferry Station 79
Quicksand Bog 80
Crocodile Rock 81
Hot Sulfur Springs 81
Herb's: Inside and Out 82
The Fisherman 83
Marko and His Hand 83
The Firefly Tree 84
Twisty Tunnel and Rat Face 85
The Skull Cave 86
The (Doltish) Dragonfly 86

7 Morningmist Valley **93**
The Haystack 94
City Gate 94
Farmer Greenberry 95
A Brief Intermission 96
The Garden 97
The Cellar 97
The Water Wheel 98
Making Sandwiches 99
Before You Leave 99

8 Highmoon Village **105**
The Drunken Dragon Tavern 107
The Gambling Octopus 108
The Altar of Doubt 109
Serving Jail Time 111
The Storekeeper 111
The Wharf 112
Mustard Island 113
How Not To Get Eaten By Cannibals 113

9 Volcania and the Center of the World **119**
Hot-Footing and Beach-Combing Across Volcania 120
Salesmen—or, When Opportunity Knocks, Half Listen 121
A Nice Sales Couple—Sort of 121
Flying Shoes Potion 122
Jessica from Miltonia 122
The Center of the World 123
Dino Troubles 124
The Stegosaurus 124
T-Rex 125
Triceratops 125
The Anchor Stone Room 127
Leaving Volcania 128

10 The Enchanted Forest **133**
The Petrified Forest 134
The Bridges of Kyrandia Kounty 134
The Footpath 135
The Tram 136

11 Alpinia **139**
Getting Uphill 139
The Shop 141
The Real Abominable Snowman 141
Rainbow Room 142
Lever Combinations and Ingredients 144
Potion Recipes 145
Crossing The Rainbow Bridge 146

12 The Wheels of Fate **149**
The Doorway 149
The Control Room 150
The Mechanic's Room (a.k.a. The Towers of Annoy) 150
Towers of Annoy Solution 151
Fixing The Missing Wheel 152

✦ BOOK 3 ✦
MALCOLM'S REVENGE 157

13 He-e-e-e's Ba-a-a-a-ck! **159**
Mission Objective 160
General Tips 160
Castle Dump 162
The Bluff 163
The Pegasus Landing 164
The Grave 164
The Dock 166
The Mime 167
The Bath House 168
The Town Arena 169
Downtown Kyrandia 170
Malcolm's Apartment 170
The Toy Factory 171
The Fish Cream Parlour 173
The Foreign Exchange Student 174
The Dairy 175
The Town Hall 176
The Cellar 177
Darm's House 178
The Catacombs 179
The Magician's Lodge (Zanthia's Place) 179
You're Under Arrest 181
Prison Situations 185
Prison Escapes 187
Leaving Kyrandia 192

14 The Isle of Cats **201**
Mission Objective 201

General Tips 202
The Dog Fort 206
Pirate Beach 209
Fluffy and The Cat Cause 210
The Altar of Cats 210
The Cat Hieroglyphics Room 211
The Colossus Ruins 213
Leaving the Isle of Cats 215

15   The Ends of the Earth **219**
Mission Objective 221
General Tips 221
Enough Already—Get Me Outta Here! 222

16   Fish World and The Underworld **227**
Mission Objective 228
Tic-Tac-Toe from Hell 228
Ed's Discount Underworld Express 229
Buddy's Garbage Dump 230
The Fish Tower 231
Perch University 232
The Underworld Entrance 233
The Royal Séance 234
The Underworld Lobby 235

17   Back to Kyrandia **241**
Mission Objective 242
Trouble in Paradise 243
The Temporary Jail 244
The Pirates and the Cat Jewels 245
Leaving Kyrandia Again 246
Town Hall 247
The Isle of Cats: Re-Do 248
Socking It To The Pirates 250
Herman's Pawn Shop 251
The Trial 252
The Great Big Finale 256

THIS BOOK IS DEDICATED
TO FELLOW PRIMA AUTHOR

STEVE SCHWARTZ

ACKNOWLEDGMENTS

Special thanks to Prima's Roger Stewart for assigning me this book, and to all of the supportive Prima team that helped get this book out: Diane Pasquetti, Brett Skogen, Mike VanMantgem, Neweleen Trebnik, and Dan Foster. Also, special thanks to designer Peter Hancik for his contribution.

At Waterside Productions, thanks once again to my distinguished agent, Matt Wagner, and to Carol Underwood and Janice Shuffield.

Lastly, the biggest thanks of all goes to Ted Morris of Westwood Studios. This book wouldn't be half the book it is without his courteous, quick, and friendly support. Ted, an Isle of Cats gem is what you are. Thanks a ton.

PREFACE

What a long, strange trip it's been. It started simply enough with Brandon in *Book 1: The Legend of Kyrandia*. Then there came Zanthia and her adventure in *Book 2: The Hand of Fate*. And now we've arrived at the most compelling book yet in this engaging saga, the conclusion to the whole Kyrandia controversy: *Book 3: Malcolm's Revenge*.

Make no mistake, this final installment is by far the most complicated Kyrandia adventure yet. Which is no doubt why you're holding this book in the first place. With it, you'll get the help you need to figure out every one of the game's trouble spots.

For those of you who are jumping into the world of Kyrandia or the first time as Malcolm the Jester, you'll be able to use this book to help figure out Kyrandia's 1 and 2 as well, if you decide to visit those titles too. That's what's nice about this series: you can play the games in any order.

MULTIPLE LEVELS OF HELP

Unlike most hint books, this one's hints and solutions are presented in a multi-layered fashion. When you find yourself stuck somewhere, look up the chapter in the table of contents that matches the chapter you're playing in the game. Next, scan the descriptive headings to locate the one that matches your current puzzle or situation.

The text under each heading contains clues that will gently nudge you toward the solution to your puzzle or problem rather than bonk you over the head with the outright answer.

If a gentle nudge isn't enough, many headings contain extra tips, as well, to lead you even closer to the solution you seek. And if that's not enough, detailed playing tips are provided as cluenotes, indicated like this.[1] Match these numbers to the corresponding endnotes at the end of the chapter for complete answers to your most puzzling questions.

MAPS

At the end of each chapter, you will find maps of the corresponding game chapter's region. Use these to find the places described in the clue text or just to simplify your navigation in certain chapters (particularly the totally obscure terrain of the Isle of Cats).

Have a great trip![2]

CLUENOTES

[1] That's right, you get the idea.

[2] P.S. Am I the only one, or have you, too, noticed that Brandywine has gone from a "he," in Kyrandia Book 1, to a "she," in Kyrandia Book 3? Weird science!

BOOK I

THE LEGEND OF
KYRANDIA

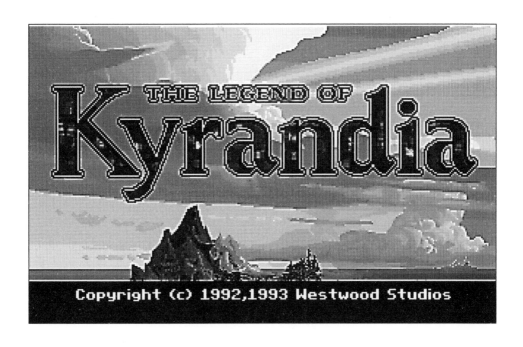

CHAPTER 1

GRAMPA'S BAD HAIR DAY

Here we are, at the beginning of it all, the commencement of Kyrandia's troubles. The first order of business is to familiarize yourself with your surroundings and with the way the game works. Roam around. Experiment. Click on anything and everything. Fortunately, this Kyrandia chapter is straightforward and makes getting into the game easy and encouraging. (It isn't until Chapter 3 that things start to get really thorny. . . .)

BRANDON'S HOMELAND

Grampa is stuck in a big way. You'll have to free him, of course, but don't spend too much time trying to do that now—there's nothing you can do to help him. Not yet, anyway. Besides, he can't even hear you! Only by playing the entire game will you find the solution to how to free Grampa.

For starters, investigate your dwelling carefully for hidden objects.[1] Look inside containers, and beneath Grampa's work bench.

Out in plain view you'll find a few items of use, including a note that Grampa penned before getting stuck in his present state and a lovely red garnet gem. (Throughout your travels in Kyrandia you'll find many gems lying around for anyone to take. You'll need them—some of them, anyway—to complete your quest. Which ones you'll need, when you'll need them, and what you'll need them for, we'll get to shortly.)

As soon as you attempt to leave your house, the tree-wall behind you will magically come to Life. Treeface will give you a short lecture on what it—and, for that matter, the world, for you must save the world of Kyrandia—expects from you.

When you're done inside, leave the house and step on the fat branch in front of your door. It works like an elevator.

Once you are grounded, wander around and get your bearings. You'll come across a number of settings and situations that are important to your quest. If you familiarize yourself with your immediate surroundings, many of the game's initial puzzles will practically figure themselves out for you.

THE WEARY WILLOW

The first sight you'll encounter to the east of Grampa's home is a sorry one—a weeping willow that's so close to death it hasn't even the strength to weep.

Notice the oddly-shaped indentation in the middle of the trunk? A perfect fit for an item you can collect a few screens to the east. The lyrics of that old '70s hit, "Raindrops keep falling on my head . . ."[2] should give you an idea of what you can do to help the ailing tree recover.

Once you've healed the tree, a young lad named Merith will appear, inviting you to a game of hide-and-seek. A little fun and games never hurt anyone . . . well, almost never. It's worth the effort, however, for this hunt will reward you with the missing piece of a rather "dull" puzzle, a little later.

BRYNN'S TEMPLE

The first time you enter your sister Brynn's stained-glass temple, the lady herself will greet you. She'll ask you for Grampa's note, which you picked up from Grampa's work bench. On first glance the note

appears blank . . . however, Brynn informs you that the note is enchanted, and so casts a spell on it to reveal Grampa's message:

"Dear Brynn: Malcolm has broken free. Soon he will come for me. Please help Brandon. Direct him toward the amulet. Use the lavender rose to key the spells. Darm and Zanthia should be able to help. Be careful, he'll try to get all of us. —Kallak"

Brynn will ask you to find her a lavender rose, with which she can create an enchantment to help you. If you didn't find a lavender rose in your early wanderings, now is a good time to hunt for one.[3]

After you've read Kallak's note, you won't need it again. Dropping it on the floor will free an empty slot in your inventory for more items.[4]

Return to Brynn with the lavender rose, and she will advise you about what to do next.

Note dropped.

POOL OF SORROW

At the Pool of Sorrow, east of your house, you'll notice it is raining teardrops. Can you catch one? Interesting shape, isn't it? It has a definite place in the story, but not in *your* tree house.[5]

FOREST ALTAR

To the extreme northwest you will encounter a dull silver altar. If your memory serves you, didn't this altar once glow with magic? Of course it did. While those lovely lavender flowers[6] adorning either side of the altar certainly help brighten the setting, something seems amiss.

Indeed, a closer look reveals a missing piece. You'll need to find a perfect fit. Perhaps a game of hide-and-seek will offer the solution.[7]

Once you fix the altar, it radiates with an intense magical glow. Brynn will tell you what the altar is waiting for when you return to her with a lavender rose.

Pool of Sorrow

Rose placed.

HERMAN AND THE RUINED BRIDGE

Southwest of Brandon's home lies a cave. Inside, a man named Herman is fretting over a broken bridge, the downfall of which he assures you he did not cause.

Attempting to cross the broken bridge with a little high-wire walking isn't a good idea.[8]

Saw placed.

When you ask Herman if he's going to fix it, he says he doesn't know how. When you suggest he get some new planks and rope, he says that the rope part is easy, but getting planks isn't, for he has nothing to cut them with. Remember that saw you found under Grampa's workbench? It sure would come in handy right now. You did take it, *didn't you*?

You won't be able to cross the bridge until Herman has finished sawing a tree and cutting some planks, and until you've finished Brynn's quest.

RETURN TO BRYNN'S TEMPLE

Once you've found a lavender rose, bring it back to Brynn. She'll perform a little magic on it and turn it into a silver rose, which she instructs you to place on the silver altar to receive the magical amulet. Do as she says and you will be mightily rewarded.[10] Before you leave Brynn, she tells you to seek Darm, who can help you with your quest.

CROSSING THE BRIDGE

Once you've received the amulet, you may return to Herman's bridge, which will be repaired now and ready to cross. Herman will tell you he lost your Grampa's saw but will offer to go find it. Don't bother waiting around for him; you don't need the saw anymore. You may now cross the bridge and proceed to *Chapter 2: Timbermist Woods and Darm.*

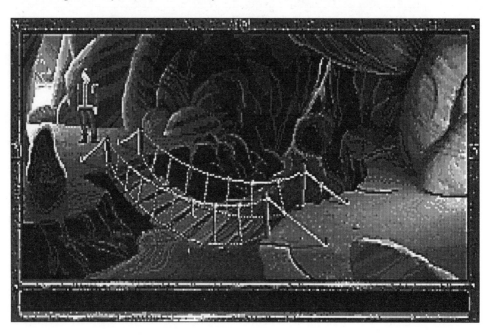

 *Items you may want to have with you at this point include some gems you picked up in your travels and the apple you found at Grampa's house.*

AT HOME

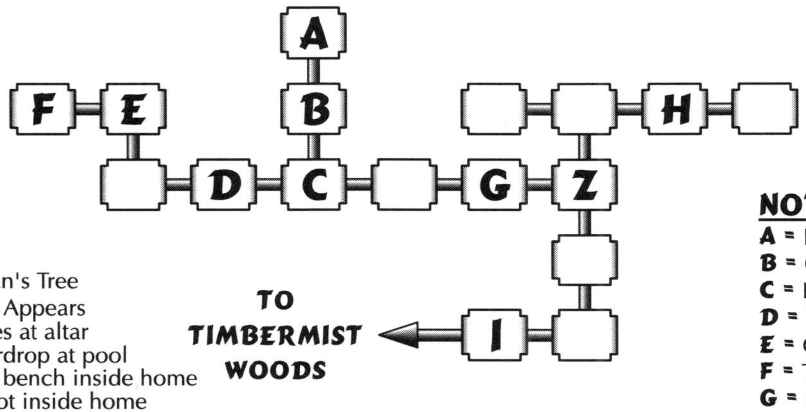
A
B
C
D
E
F
G
H
I
Z
TO
TIMBERMIST
WOODS

MISC.

X = Herman's Tree
Z = Perdot Appears
Purple roses at altar
Crystal teardrop at pool
Saw under bench inside home
Apple in pot inside home

NOTABLE SCENES

A = Inside Home
B = Outside Home
C = Below Home
D = Willow
E = Outside Temple
F = Temple
G = Pool Of Sorrow
H = Silver Altar
I = Ruined Bridge

CLUENOTES

[1] Items of use: an apple in the urn beside your bed, Grampa's saw hidden beneath the work table, a garnet gem from the work table, and a note, also on the table.

[2] Click on the falling rain drops at the Pool of Sorrow, located to the right of Brandon's home, to catch a teardrop. Give the teardrop to the sickly willow tree to save it.

[3] Situated to the far east of Brandon's home there is an altar, with lavender roses growing on either side of it. Go ahead and pluck one, and bring it to Brynn.

[4] For those of you who don't like to litter (and who are perhaps fond of playing with matches), try dropping the note onto the incense burner's flame.

[5] Give the teardrop to the weeping willow tree.

[6] Go ahead and pluck a flower—it's the lavender variety that Brynn asked you to find.

[7] After you heal the weeping willow tree, young Merith will lure you into a little game of chase, promising to show you a marble he "found." Catch the little thief, then replace the Altar's missing purple marble with the one Merith lets you have.

[8] Though it is lethal, it's fun to watch Brandon attempt to cross the rope. Make sure you save your game first, though, so you can resume where you left off. Er, fell off.

[9] Herman won't finish fixing the bridge until you possess the amulet, which Brynn will tell you how to get once you bring her the lavender rose. You'll need the amulet to advance to the game's next chapter, which begins on the other side of the bridge.

[10] (If you haven't repaired the Altar yet, go back and heal the weeping willow tree first.) The Altar will crackle with lightning and consume the silver rose—at the same time, a magic amulet will appear in your inventory, in the bottom right corner.

CHAPTER 2

TIMBERMIST WOODS AND DARM

This chapter is a fun one, especially the parts where Darm and his purple dragon friend, Brandywine, banter like a silly TV sitcom couple. You can work out the chapter's most formidable puzzle, the birthstone puzzle, with a little patience and a lot of experimentation.

The Timbermist Woods

Be warned, however, that not all of Chapter 2 is fun and games. Evil lurks just around the corner—a corner that you will turn very soon.

THE WIZARD DARM

Finding Darm is easy—his straw-roof hut is the first location you'll encounter when you cross Herman's bridge and exit the cave.

Inside Darm's hut, you'll find the senile old Wizard himself, as well as his enormous, pithy, purple dragon, Brandywine. After a little bantering, Darm will ask you to find him a quill, so that he can write. Until you bring him a quill, Darm won't have any further business with you.

The quest for a quill is, like most of the game's quests, easier to complete after you've explored your immediate surroundings. Go ahead, wander around Timbermist Woods a little and see what you find.[1]

When you give Darm a quill he'll write you a message on a magic scroll. Put it in your inventory for now; you'll need it later.[2]

Inside Darm's abode

Next, Darm will send you on a birthstone puzzle quest . . . but we're getting ahead of ourselves a bit. We'll figure that one out after you find Darm's quill.

Since you will eventually need several gems to solve the birthstone puzzle, stockpile any that you collect near the Marble Altar, so that you can make more room in your knapsack for more gems and items.

OLD NOLBY AND THE OLDEST OAK TREE

This old-timer, hogging the entire bench, offers a direct clue to solving Darm's quill quest. Listen closely, and Nolby will say something about the last living songbird.[3] (And, no, the bird drinking at the bird bath isn't the last living songbird. Wander around; you'll find him nearby.)

SONGBIRD'S NEST

Beneath the hurt songbird's nest, you'll find a walnut. Take it. You'll need it to solve Darn's quill quest puzzle.[4] Don't bother trying to help the bird just yet—you'll be more useful to it after you've taken care of business in Deadwood Glade.

Walnut placed.

THE BUBBLING SPRING

There's more here than meets the eye. Notice how crystal clear the water is? And those yellow flowers are pretty, aren't they?[5]

DEADWOOD GLADE

So, you've found Deadwood Glade. Now we're getting somewhere. Sad-looking place, isn't it? It sure could use a little sprucing up. Notice that huge hole in the ground? No, it isn't home to a dog-sized gopher. It is rather accommodating, though. Have you anything in your inventory that you might drop in the hole?

There are three items that you need to plant in the hole, and none of them are gems. All three items can be found in nearby places.[6] The ground will shake each time you drop in one of the correct items. After you plant all three items in the hole, something fabulous will happen.[7]

THE YELLOW AMULET GEM

Once you've revived Deadwood Glade, a yellow gem will appear in your amulet. Go ahead and touch it. Invigorating, isn't it? And yes, this yellow amulet gem will indeed come in handy if you—or another living creature—become injured.[8] Tweet tweet.

When you touch the yellow gem to activate its healing magic, it will fade for a short period of time while it recharges. Try to stay out of trouble until it glows again. A poisonous bite, for example, will knock you dead in a few short turns if you don't heal yourself immediately with the yellow gem.

THE BIRTHSTONE QUEST

According to Darm, you'll need to place your birthstones in some sort of plate. You'll need to place them in a particular order, according to the Seasons. Figuring out the right order to place the gems is the hardest part of this particular puzzle.

Darm did give you one clue: Summer is the first season, and the first stone that you'll need to place, which represents that season, is hidden somewhere nearby. It's not very easy to find, but here's another clue: What season comes before Summer? *In* the answer to this question is where you'll find the Sunstone.[9]

Nine additional birthstones are scattered around Timbermist Woods. Collect them as you find them, and store them at the Marble Altar, which is where you'll use them.

THE MARBLE ALTER

Low and behold, a plate. As Darm said, this plate is where you'll place the birthstones in a particular order. You know that Summer comes first, and by now you've probably found the Sunstone. That leaves Fall, Winter, and Spring.

After you place the first birthstone—the Sunstone—the first indentation in the altar will glow, indicating a correct match.

The second and third birthstones vary from game to game. The only way to figure out which stones come second and third is by trying different stones. Save your game after you place the first birthstone, then, once you figure out which stone comes second, restore your game to the last save, place the second birthstone, and save again. Repeat this process for the third stone.

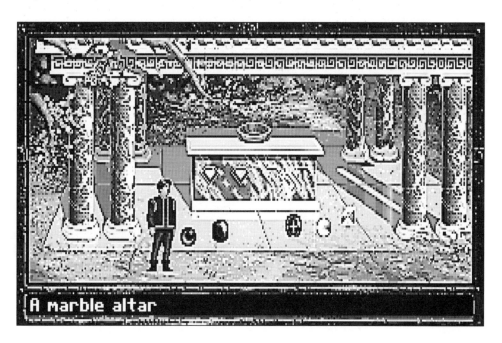

A marble altar

The forth stone is always the same in every game. Here's a clue: This one literally grows on trees and is very red—as red as red gets.[10]

After you've placed all four gems in the correct order on the plate, the plate will sparkle and transform itself into another item.[11] Take the new item.

If you run out of stones while trying to solve the birthstone puzzle, wander around and find more. Don't forget to look in the area east of Darm's hut—outside the cave you came through to reach Timbermist Woods in the first place. It's easy to overlook and often has one or more gems lying around. Also: you may need to return to your Home Area to search for additional stones if you are unable to find the ones you need in Timbermist Woods.

The Timbermist Woods

Don't bother trying to steal the Emerald in the Statue south of Darm's. It's a permanent fixture here in Timbermist Woods, so hands off.

THE RUBY TREE

Pick one of these, and you'll get bitten by a snake. A deadly snake. Worry not. You can heal yourself . . . can't you? If you haven't figured out how to heal yourself, then don't pick one of these just yet.[12] Wait until you can heal yourself. (See Deadwood Glade.) Then come back and take one — you'll need one for the birthstone puzzle.

Ow! That snake bit me!

DANGER

A ruby tree

SERPENT'S GROTTO

Quite a chilling place, isn't it? (Suggestion: Saved your game lately? If not, now is a good time to do so.) You may visit here all you like, but try to enter the cave and you will meet up with your greatest foe—Malcolm. Yes, folks, here he is, the no-good jester who's to blame for all of Kyrandia's troubles.[13] After you two exchange various insults directed at one another's mothers, Malcolm will throw a quick test of courage your way.

A word of warning: Don't back down to Malcolm. Which is to say, fire back at him whatever he fires at you—immediately—or else you're through! Get the point?[14]

Stand up to Malcolm and he'll take off inside the cave, which he seals shut with a great wall of ice. Don't panic. There is a way inside, if you have a certain item and know how to use it. Perhaps Darm can offer some advice?

SAY GOOD-BYE TO DARM

Before you go chasing after Malcolm—providing you've figured out a way to break through his icy barrier—drop in on Darm to say good-bye. When you tell him you've solved the birthstone puzzle, he'll comment on your new flute. He'll ask if you've practiced with it yet. Well, have you? It *is* rather shrill, isn't it?

Darm will instruct you to seek Zanthia, an alchemist. He'll offer some advice, but pay no further mind to him. Listen to Brandywine. He'll explain that Zanthia can be found on the other side of

Shadowrealm, a dark and twisted labyrinth, which is accessed though the cave in Serpent's Grotto. Now, if only you could break through Malcolm's icy blockade.[15]

Of course, you may already have shattered his brittle attempt at keeping you out of Shadowrealm. After him!

Any gems you've gathered or flowers you've plucked can be stockpiled outside the cave (or inside Shadowrealm, at the Chasm of Everfall), where they will be easy to get to later, to take with you into Faeriewood. Also: You can leave the flute behind; you won't need it anymore.

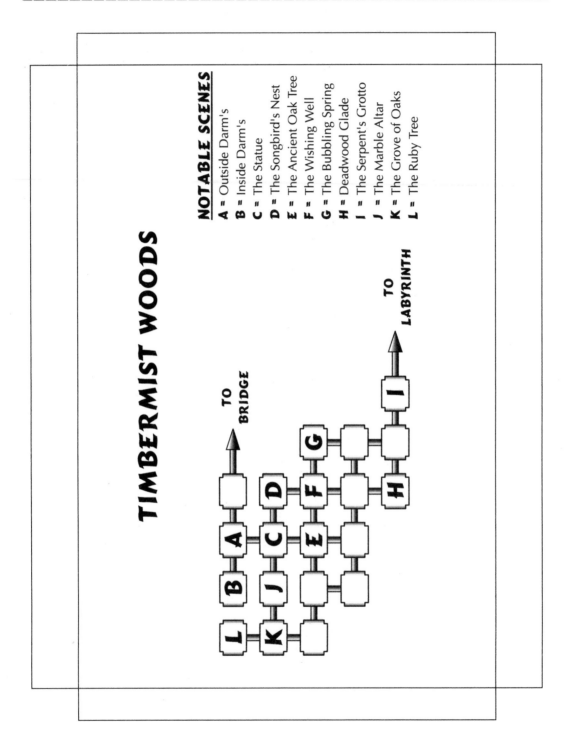

TIMBERMIST WOODS

NOTABLE SCENES

A = Outside Darm's
B = Inside Darm's
C = The Statue
D = The Songbird's Nest
E = The Ancient Oak Tree
F = The Wishing Well
G = The Bubbling Spring
H = Deadwood Glade
I = The Serpent's Grotto
J = The Marble Altar
K = The Grove of Oaks
L = The Ruby Tree

TO BRIDGE

TO LABYRINTH

CLUENOTES

1 You can't possibly need a clue already! Go have a look around first, then come back for clues later.

2 You'll use the scroll Darm gives you in Chapter 3 and again in Chapter 4. When to use it? Hint: When things get too hot to handle, that's the time to cast this spell on yourself.

3 Nolby says that the last living songbird is ailing and needs to be healed. Go find the ailing bird.

4 No, it isn't time for an outright solution to the quill puzzle just yet. Keep wandering around, until you find two more seedy items.

5 Pick one now and it will come in handy later.

6 You've head the saying, "You plant potatoes, you get potatoes," right? In this case, planting something other than potatoes—three things, in fact—will yield more than French Fries. The three things are the walnut beneath the injured songbird's nest, an acorn picked from the grove of oaks, and the pine cone lying on the ground in the Dark Forest.

7 A nutty, talking pseudobushia tree will sprout from the ground. To express its gratitude for restoring life to the once dead Deadwood Glade, the talking bush will kiss you. And what a kiss! Suddenly, the yellow gem in your amulet is glowing. Now why is that?

8 While old Nolby is rather ailing, he's not the injured creature we're concerned with here. It's the nested songbird that needs a little magic healing. Once you heal it, it will fly off, leaving behind a feather, which, according to legend—Kyrandian and otherworldian—qualifies as a quill. Give it to Darm.

9 That is a tricky clue, isn't it? Yes, Spring is the answer. And in the Bubbling Spring you'll find a Sunstone, the first birthstone you'll need for solving the birthstone puzzle. While you're here, help yourself to a yellow tulip. It will come in handy later for creating a potion.

10 As in, ruby red. You'll find plenty of these gems in the far northwestern region, however taking one will present its own particularly nasty challenge. Make sure you save your game before you try snatching one.

11 A flute, perfect for hitting ear-shattering high-highs.

12 After you pick a Ruby and get bitten by the snake, touch the glowing yellow gem on your amulet to heal yourself. Make sure you pick a Ruby only when your yellow amulet gem is glowing and ready to use. If it isn't glowing and you pick a ruby, you'll die of snake poisoning before you have time to heal yourself with the gem.

13 Then again, he's not all that bad. After all, had he not turned Kyrandia upside-down, we wouldn't be having so much fun chasing him down and solving all of these puzzles, would we?

14 Which is to say, explicitly: Click on the knife that he throws at you when the arrow cursor reappears, or else he'll finish you off then and there, and the game will end. And don't try to save your game first—Malcolm will consider that your fair move and will hit you with his deadly magic.

15 Well, have you tried your flute? No, throwing it at the ice wall won't create any startling break-throughs. However, playing your flute, by touching it on yourself, will have the right effect on the ice wall. Darn tootin'. That done, you can ditch the flute—you won't need it again to complete the game.

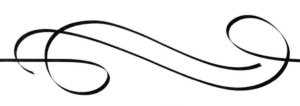

CHAPTER 3

SHADOWREALM LABYRINTH

That last chapter wasn't so tough, was it? But things can't stay easy for you, now could they? Of course not. What fun would that be? Here it is, your first real nightmare: Shadowrealm. This place is huge, but that's not the problem. The problem is that it's very dark here. Fireberries will help provide some light, but only for three turns at a time. Luckily, you're not completely in the dark. With the map provided and some strategic plucking and laying of fireberry bushes, you'll come out of Shadowrealm a little stronger, a little wiser, and a lot less afraid of the dark.

A natural mineral pool

While you may be tempted to leave Shadowrealm after you've helped the will-o-wisps, don't go until you've visited the Volcanic River.

NATURAL MINERAL POOL

The first site in here is a pretty one. Stalagmites and crystal water pools give the illusion that all is wonderful. Don't let this first impression fool you. Quick lesson: Shadowrealm is a dark and dangerous place. The real danger here is shadow wraiths. You can't see them because they only come out in the dark. Pitch black dark, to be exact. That's why you need to use the fireberries to light your way through the labyrinth in an orderly and straightforward fashion.

The map at the end of this chapter will help you find your way. Pay particular attention to the fireberry locations. Using those locations, you can proceed from one to the next, lighting your way as you go by dropping fireberries. Eventually, you want to wind your way to the upper right corner, where you'll find the last rock necessary to open the gate.

WHY AM I HERE, ANYWAY? (OR, THE IRON GATE)

To get out, of course. For as soon as you cross the cavern with the iron gate, the gate will slam shut behind you, locking you inside.

How to get out? One look at the gate tells you that it is controlled by the suspended dish and counterweight mechanism. You'll need to toss some heavy objects into the dish to balance the counterweight and, thus, reopen the gate.

Better start searching for some heavy objects.[1]

A treacherous crossing

FIREBERRY BUSHES

Fireberries last *three turns* when you carry them. Which is to say, when you pick a fireberry, you can go three screens in any direction and the fireberry will light your way. After the third screen, or turn, the berry will burn out. The idea is to pick and explore from one bush to the next, without winding up in the dark. There is a trick to keeping the fireberries from burning out: Drop them. That's right, drop them on the ground behind you as you go, and they'll stay lit, providing both light to see by and markers to gauge your place in the maze.

Make sure you pick three fireberries every time you encounter a fireberry bush. Drop one berry in each passage between each fireberry bush location. That way you'll be able to see on your way out.

THE CHASM OF EVERFALL

As its name implies, here lies a chasm. And everyone knows chasms were made to be crossed. You'll get out of here by crossing one—but not until you've solved the gate puzzle and performed a little task back in Timbermist Woods using an object that you will find deep in the labyrinth, in the Cavern of Twilight.[2]

TIP *You may stockpile items you're carrying by the gate or at the Chasm of Everfall and retrieve them later. However, make sure you take along the spell Darm gave you when you venture into the labyrinth, as you'll need it later.[3]*

Sapphire dropped.

THE PANTHEON OF MOONLIGHT

Notice it's light in here? Those two floating things that look like dandelion puffs are actually will-o-wisps, which float and give off light. Listen closely to what they say.

They offer to help you, but only if you help them first. They want you to complete the construction of the Pantheon of Moonlight. To do so, you'll need an item found a little farther along the way, in . . .

The Pantheon of Moonlight

THE CAVERN OF TWILIGHT

Considering what you've been through here, wandering aimlessly through a scary dark maze, what is the one thing you wish for more than anything else?[4] Using what you find here, your wish can come true—if you use the object in the right place. (Hint: A little backtracking, to a previous chapter, will be in order.[5]) Providing, that is, you find the object in question in the first place. Actually, there are two items here that you'll need to take—the first one is the object we were just discussing, and the second one is a rock, lying on the stone ground to the right of the screen.

THE EMERALD CAVE

As you make your way to the final rock, you'll pass through the Emerald Cave, all green and glowing. There are two emeralds here; however, you only need to take one. Providing, of course, you have

The Cavern of Twilight

room in your inventory. You have been careful about leaving items stockpiled, to pick up again later, haven't you?

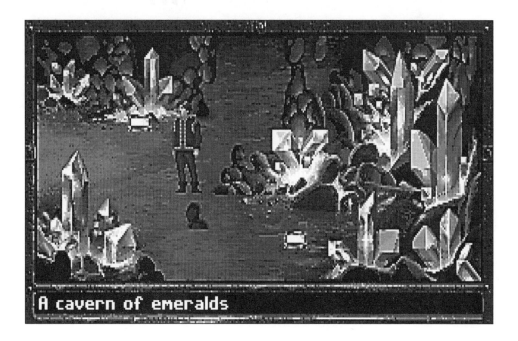

A cavern of emeralds

UNLOCKING THE GATE

Once you've made your way back to the locked gate with five rocks, you're ready to get the heck outta here.[6] But not so fast. You'll need to return—remember that Chasm of Everfall we checked out earlier? That's ultimately where you're headed. But first, there's a wish you need to fulfill, one that will help both you and those will-o-wisps you met earlier. Go back to Timbermist Woods and take care of business.

Well, have you figured out what to do to make your wish come true? WELL?[7] Once you cast your wish, a Moonstone will appear. Take it, and use it to help the will-o-wisps.

BACK TO SHADOWREALM

You're thinking: Oh no, no more labyrinth! Remember, the only way to get to Faeriewood and find the Alchemist Zanthia is through Shadowrealm.

We're almost done here. Did you help the will-o-wisps? If not, do so now. They'll reward you with a special amulet gem.

THE PURPLE AMULET GEM

Indeed, your fear of the dark is cured. When you activate the purple gem by touching it, you'll turn into a will-o-wisp yourself, not only full of sight-giving light, but also able to float in the air and cross impossible spans.[8] Feels nice, doesn't it? Ready to leave? Hold on. Not quite yet. There's still one more thing you need to do here in Shadowrealm.

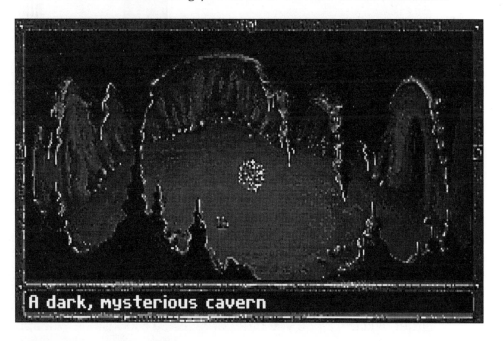

A dark, mysterious cavern

VOLCANIC RIVER

Have you found this hot and fiery place yet? It's located in the lower right corner of the Shadowrealm labyrinth. It's advisable to save your game before trying to cross the lava chasm on foot.[9] Indeed, you'll need to get across somehow, for there's an item on the other side that you must retrieve. Hint: There's an item you received earlier, during your travels in Timbermist Woods, that will come in handy now.[10]

Scroll placed.

After you've crossed the Volcanic River and obtained the item[11] on the other side, turn yourself into a will-o-wisp again and return to the Chasm of Everfall.

Iron Key taken.

CROSSING TO SAFETY (SORT OF)

Now that you know how to fly, you may safely cross the Chasm of Everfall and proceed to Faeriewood, where you will seek Zanthia the Alchemist. Yes, the crossing part is indeed safe . . . but what's hanging around on the other side is going to start things off with a bang, so to speak.

Before you cross the chasm to Faeriewood, gather up any gems and flowers you have stockpiled here or in Timbermist Woods earlier. You'll need these items to create potions in Chapter 4.

Take one fireberry from the room just south of the Chasm of Everfall with you before you cross the chasm. On the other side, drop the berry in the one and only dark cavern between the chasm and Faeriewood. A fireberry here will keep the room light for when you return to it later, keeping those pesky wraiths at bay.

Emerald placed.

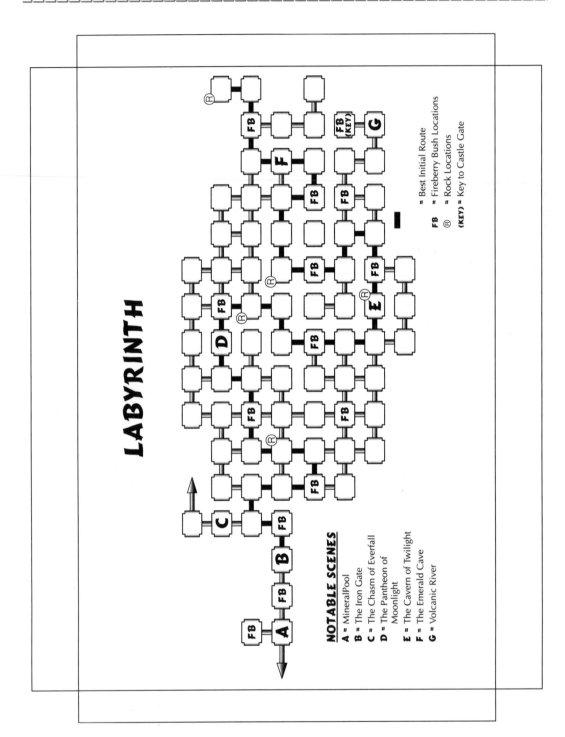

LABYRINTH

NOTABLE SCENES

A = MineralPool
B = The Iron Gate
C = The Chasm of Everfall
D = The Pantheon of Moonlight
E = The Cavern of Twilight
F = The Emerald Cave
G = Volcanic River

= Best Initial Route
FB = Fireberry Bush Locations
Ⓡ = Rock Locations
(KEY) = Key to Castle Gate

CLUENOTES

1 Rocks. Five of them, to be exact, which you'll place on the dish in order to weigh it down sufficiently to open the gate.

2 A coin, which you will use back in Timbermist Woods. Where, we won't reveal just yet. You have enough to worry about as it is, just finding those rocks and getting that gate open.

3 At the Volcanic River.

4 Light, of course. If you had a flashlight, or something that works like a flashlight, you wouldn't have to worry about fireberries anymore.

5 See cluenote 2. And no, that doesn't mean placing the coin on the altar in the Pantheon of Moonlight. You'll use the coin somewhere else to create another object, which you will place in the base of the altar Pantheon of Moonlight.

6 To unlock the gate, stack the five rocks on the suspended dish.

7 Well, well, well, the Wishing Well seems like a pretty good place to make a wish by dropping in the coin you found in the Cavern of Twilight.

8 A word of warning: The will-o-wisp spell lasts for a certain amount of time — usually long enough for you to get from one end of the labyrinth to the other end. If, however, the will-o-wisp spell wears off when you're in a dark location, you will be eaten by the wraiths. All the more reason to place those fireberries between bush locations, as described earlier, in case you make a wrong turn.

9 To put it another way, don't do it. You can't make it across. It will take magic to get across this hot spot.

10 The only way to get across is by casting the spell Darm gave you. Cast it on yourself, and the Volcanic River will turn to ice, safe to cross.

11 An Iron Key.

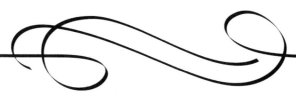

CHAPTER 4

FAERIEWOOD AND ZANTHIA

Although your first venture into the vast Faeriewood realm will serve up a surprising lesson from the school of hard knocks, there is much wonder here. Zanthia the Alchemist has more than a few tricks up her sleeve, thank goodness, and once more you'll run into your archenemy, the menacing Malcolm. As in Shadowrealm, you'll cover lots of ground in Faeriewood that has little or no bearing on your ultimate quest. But with a clear head and a keen eye on managing your inventory and learning a new trade, you'll leave

A cavernous entrance

Faeriewood stronger and more capable than ever—and ready for your final showdown with Malcolm.

The following locations are listed in the most effective order for solving Faeriewood's many challenging puzzles. This is one section where there's little rhyme or reason to solving puzzles, so don't feel bad if you get frustrated in Faeriewood. Also: Pay particular attention to the "Important Tip" at the end of this chapter, for it describes which items you must have in your inventory in order to continue to the last chapter and finish the game.

KNOCKING SOME SENSE

When you emerge on the other side of the chasm in Faeriewood, the world looks divine. There's even a shiny red apple here. Go on, take it.[1] Then wander around. Before long, though, you'll encounter some trouble. There's nothing you can do to avoid it, so just take your knocks like a good prince, and next thing you know you'll wind up where you belong. Prince . . . did someone say . . . Prince?

Dark forest

ZANTHIA'S LAB

Waking up in a strange place has its advantages, especially when the place you awaken in is where you intended to wind up in the first place. Meet Zanthia. After you got knocked in the head, she kindly dragged you from the woods to her lab. During your brief chat with Zanthia, she says something about you being a Prince. Pressed for an explanation, she changes the subject, sending you out to fill a flask with magic water from the fountain. This shouldn't be too hard . . . after all, there is a fountain just a little to the west.

You can drop all of your gems and flowers here, since this is the place where you're going to use them shortly.

Beware of those watchful eyes outside Zanthia's lab. You don't want to mess with this sucker. To put it another way, it's okay to look, but don't touch.[2]

Tulip dropped.

THE FOUNTAIN AND MALCOLM

So much for simplicity. Look who's here: Malcolm. When you tell
him that you simply want to get some water and then you'll be on
your way, he decides to play nasty and disable the fountain by
snatching off one of its magical crystal orbs. Bummer. Well, like
Malcolm says, it's time for a little hide and seek. There's no use going
back to Zanthia for help—you're on your own for this one. Clue: In
the heat of the moment, a little magic will cool things down.

Now is as good a time as any to take in your surroundings while
you search for the missing orb.[3] There are a few sites of interest, all of
which lie west of Zanthia's lab.

Once you find the missing orb, replace it on the fountain. The
fountain will come back to life. Get some water for Zanthia, as she
requested.

A ruined fountain

If you're feeling a little thirsty, go ahead and help yourself to a little drink. Heck, even if you *aren't* thirsty have a drink anyway; you'll be glad you did.[4]

Magical Water placed.

THE BURNING TREE

Like they say, fight fire with fire. Or is it fight fire with water? That seems to make more sense, but you have no water—Malcolm made it all vanish. Then again, there is water at the Sparkling Waterfall. Even so, you *already* have water available to you, if you really think about it. No, it's not in the form you'd naturally expect, but it will work nonetheless to put out the fire.[5]

Scroll taken.

BACK TO ZANTHIA WITH THE MAGIC WATER

When you return to Zanthia's with the magic water, she'll dump it into her cauldron, and, while she's stirring the pot, she'll reveal to you a long-hidden secret: That you, Brandon, are the Prince of Kyrandia. The bad news is that this clown you keep running into, Malcolm, is the monster who killed your parents, King William and

Katherine. Malcolm broke free of the magical bonds that once held him and took off with the Kyragem. Only you, the rightful heir to the throne, can stop Malcolm.

Heavy stuff to deal with on such short notice, but time's a-wasting, Prince Brandon. Zanthia says she will concoct a potion for you, but she'll need some blueberries, which she asks you to go find.[6]

Blueberries placed.

When you return, Zanthia will have vanished. Now, where could she have gone? Search her lab closely for hints—a clue to her whereabouts lies right under your nose![7]

THE OTHER SIDE OF FAERIEWOOD

A secret passage in Zanthia's lab will lead you to the Other Side of Faeriewood. There's mostly forest over here, but you'll also find two important locales. At the first site, you will find the Crystals of

Alchemy. Notice those bottle-shaped indentations in either crystal? Remember them. We'll come back to them later.

The Crystals of Alchemy

The second site, the Tropical Lagoon, is where you will find a platform with two golden, winged-horse statues on either side. There are also some exotic red orchids growing here. Take two of these.[8]

The Tropical Lagoon also happens to be your gateway out of Faeriewood. But don't think of leaving until you've learned how to mix up some potions for yourself. What? You haven't forgotten that that was why Zanthia requested blueberries, have you? Back to the Lab with you.

BUBBLE, BUBBLE, TOIL AND TROUBLESOME POTIONS

Zanthia *was* going to make a potion for you with those blueberries you brought back for her, but now that she's gone you're the master of the Lab, friend.

How to begin? Well, there is a bubbling cauldron here which, besides using it to do her laundry, one can only assume Zanthia uses to create potions. And she did ask you for some blueberries, right? Go ahead . . . toss them in.

The water turns blue. When you try to fill a vial with the light blue water, though, you are informed that the potion is only *half* complete. It's going to take another item to complete the potion. Still have those gems you've been carrying around? Hint: Similar colors go together when it comes to making potions.[9]

When you're done, you should have a blue potion, a red potion, and a yellow potion, each in it's own little flask. Of these three colored potions, you'll need a second bottle of one of them, for a total of four potions.[10]

Empty Flask dropped.

 *If you find that you need a particular color of gem but don't have one, you may need to go back to Timbermist Woods to get one or more.*

 *Empty potion flasks appear in Zanthia's lab when you exit for a moment then come back in.*

MAKING NEW POTIONS

Now, what the heck do you do with them? None of them is meant to be consumed as it is. Rather, each must be combined with another to create a new potion. For this alchemy you do not use the cauldron.

Have you visited the Crystals of Alchemy yet? Notice the shape of the potion flasks? Get the hint? With a little experimenting, you can combine your four potions to create two different colored potions.[11]

Once you've created your two new potions, they're ready to use—but only in the right place, at the right time. Figuring out this puzzle is difficult. One way to get a clue of each potion's use is to save your game, then drink each one to read the description of the feeling you get.[12] After you've tested each potion, restore your game to the point before you drank the potions and then continue with your journey.

If this method doesn't help you figure out where you'll need the new potions, don't worry, you'll find out *shortly*.

THE ROYAL CHALICE

Floating in mid-air is the golden Royal Chalice. Jumping or changing into a will-o-wisp won't bring the Chalice any closer into your hands. (By the way, don't bother with the Royal Chalice until you've created the new potions, as described above.)

It's going to take magic to get this cup down. The magic you need will come from your amulet. Has another of your amulet's gems come alive yet? If not, there's something in Faeriewood that you'll need to consume in order to make your amulet's next gem glow. Hint: It's not a potion that you must consume; however an empty flask will be necessary to acquire the liquid you must drink.[13]

After you manage to free the Chalice of its magic bond, it's only free for an instant, because a little creature bursts onto the scene, snatches the Chalice, and takes off before you can lay a hand on it. Catch that little geek (or whatever he is)!

Dark forest

A NATURAL CLEARING AND FAUN'S HOME

In the clearing south of the Magic Fountain is a large tree with a little door in its base. You can do nothing here until you've freed the Chalice one screen to the west. Once you have, you'll need to get in that tiny door, for surely that's where the little creature who snatched the Chalice is hiding. Getting inside is easy as long as you've concocted the right potion.[14]

Inside, the little creature Faun says he'll give you the Chalice but only if you give him something good first. Hint: While he doesn't like the taste of alfalfa, there is an item he'd like to have that he can't normally get because he isn't tall enough to pick one.[15]

Apple taken.

LEAVING FAERIEWOOD

Once you've got the Chalice, you're ready to leave Faeriewood by
way of the Tropical Lagoon, located at the far northeast of the Other
Side of Faeriewood.

*Important: Once you leave Faeriewood, you will not be able to return.
Before you go, make sure you have the Iron Key[16], the Royal Chalice,
and a flower. One of the red orchids growing at the Tropical Lagoon will
do nicely. With these three items in your inventory, you are ready to
leave Faeriewood. (These are the only items you will need to take with
you, so feel free to leave behind the spell Darm gave you or any gems
or items you've gathered.)*

Crossing the lagoon will require a little helpful magic.[17] Before you
do anything too daring, make sure you save your game. Then take
flight, young Prince, for it's time to face your nemesis.

Orange Potion taken.

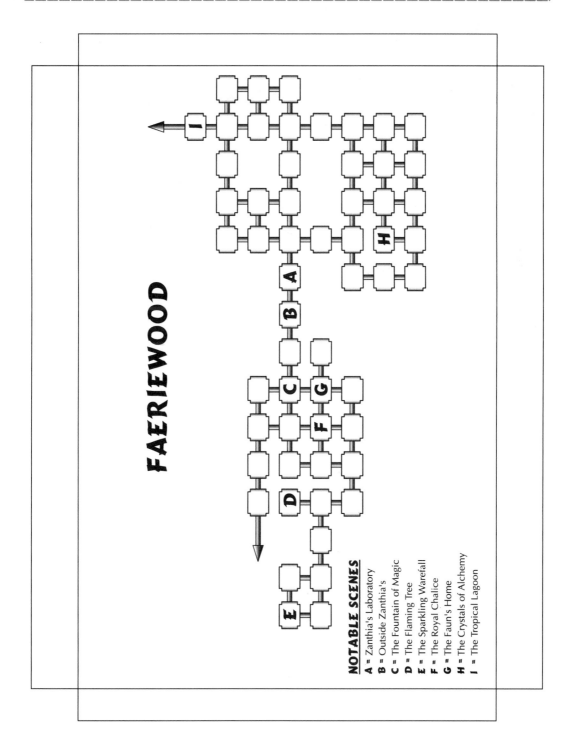

FAERIEWOOD

NOTABLE SCENES

A = Zanthia's Laboratory
B = Outside Zanthia's
C = The Fountain of Magic
D = The Flaming Tree
E = The Sparkling Warefall
F = The Royal Chalice
G = The Faun's Home
H = The Crystals of Alchemy
I = The Tropical Lagoon

CLUENOTES

1 Just because you take the apple doesn't mean you need to eat it. Hang on to it—it will come in handy later.

2 These roving eyes belong to a huge, hungry frog who will eat you if you get too close.

3 The orb is hidden in the Flaming Tree.

4 Drinking a flask of the Magic Water will activate the blue gem on your amulet. The blue gem will allow you to dispel certain enchantments.

5 Cast the spell Darm gave you at the Flaming Tree to extinguish the fire. The orb that Malcolm hid will be revealed. Take it and return it to the Fountain to revive the magic water. You can throw away the magic spell that Darm gave you now, you won't need it anymore.

6 Have you've been to the Sparkling Waterfall yet? Go there, and ye shall find what ye seeks: Blueberries.

7 Notice the rug has been moved? Check it out.

8 You'll need two red orchids to concoct two red potions back at Zanthia's Lab. You'll need a third one when you leave Faeriewood later, but you can wait until just before you depart to take that one.

9 Which is to say, blue goes with blue, yellow with yellow (or green), and red with red. Another way to look at it: Blueberries and blue gems mix. Red flowers and red gems mix. And yellow flowers and yellow or green gems mix.

10 Red. You''ll need two red potions.

11 Place one potion flask in each Crystal indentation. Two potions create one new potion. To create the new potions you'll need, do the following: 1) mix a blue potion with a red potion, to create a Purple potion, and 2) mix a red potion with a yellow potion, to create an Orange potion. Don't bother mixing blue and yellow potions to create a green potion. It's poisonous.

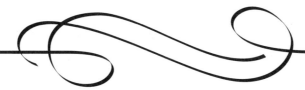

12 The Orange potion tastes like alfalfa. There is a particular animal that eats alfalfa, and consuming the Orange potion in this inanimate creature's company will help you leave Faeriewood. The Purple potion will cause you to shrink to a very small size. Do you remember seeing a place where this height may be just the right size for gaining access to a small dwelling?

13 Go to the Fountain of Magic and collect some of its water in an empty flask. Drink the water, and the blue gem in your amulet will glow. The blue gem will allow you to dispel certain enchantments, such as magic that causes the Chalice to float in thin air.

14 Drink the purple potion to shrink in size, then open the tiny door and go inside.

15 Give the kid an apple and he'll tell you where he hid the Chalice. If you need an apple, there is one outside the cave, where you exited Shadowrealm labyrinth. There was also one in your Grampa's home at the beginning of the game, remember? In the event that you've eaten both of these apples, another one can be found in the woods in the Other Side of Faeriewood.

16 The Iron Key is hidden in Shadowrealm Labyrinth. See Volcanic River topic in Chapter 3.

17 You're thinking "will-o-wisp will get me there," right? Wrong. For fun, though, save your game and try it anyway. After a laugh, restore your game and then drink the orange potion—the alfalfa juice—to turn yourself into a winged horse.

CHAPTER 5

CASTLE KYRANDIA AND THE BIG SHOWDOWN

You've made it this far, Brandon, and it hasn't been easy, but the worst is yet to come. For here, in Castle Kyrandia, you'll face the

A dark island

murderous Malcolm once and for all.[1] With some clever thinking and acting, though, you'll get a chance to save the Kyragem and restore order to the once-peaceful Kyrandia Lands.

A MISTY GRAVE (MAMA MIA)

The first location you'll come to after you arrive on the Island is the grave of your murdered parents. You wish there was something you could do to honor their memory. Actually, there is. The solution to this puzzle isn't a thorny one.[2] Laying something on the grave will fulfill your wish.

When the correct offering is placed on the grave, your mother's spirit will appear. She will tell you that you must heal the Kyragem and reclaim the throne. To do this, she says, you will need a Royal Chalice,[3] which you already posses.

She'll also cast some sort of magic spell on you that will activate the fourth and final gem in your amulet, the red gem.

Go ahead and experiment with your newest gem if you like, but remember, once you use it, you'll need to give it time to recharge before you can use it again.[4]

THE CASTLE GATE

Those concrete gargoyles are scary enough when they're frozen, but watch out when they come to life. They'll do just that if you get too close to the gate, which, incidentally, is locked.[5] In two seconds flat, they'll zap you with green acid and put you out of the game for good. Unless, that is, you can sneak past them unnoticed. Have you visited your parents' grave yet? Have you met your mother's spirit? If not, go back there and seek her help.[6]

MALCOLM REVISITED

Well look who it is—that jovial, murdering jester, Malcolm. After some taunting, Malcolm tells you that you're welcome to stay here in his

(your!) humble abode; however, you'll have to observe two house rules. The first is not to disturb his daily nap. The second is to keep away from the Kyra-Vault. Of course, you'll break both rules in due time.

Before Malcolm vanishes, he mentions that Herman, the fellow whom you helped repair the bridge between your Grandpa's house and Timbermist Woods, has taken up residence here as well, as Malcolm's servant. Malcolm says that Herman is eager to give back the saw that you loaned him, so keep a watchful eye out for the brainwashed Herman and his gnashing saw-teeth.[7]

Inside the castle, which has a first level and a second level (plus a secret area, which you can uncover somewhere on the first level), there are a number of important rooms to locate. For starters, stay on the main floor—the one you entered—and wander around.

THE GREAT HALL

Inside the Great Hall, with its enormous dining table and candelabra, you can access adjacent rooms by clicking directly on their open doorways. Notice the huge locked double-doors at the back of the Great Hall. Your main quest here is to find a way through those locked doors.[8] Better start searching.

THE KITCHEN

Northeast of the Great Hall lies the Kitchen. It's a mess in here, but search carefully and you'll find an item of use.[9]

THE LIBRARY

There are two points of interest here. First, have you approached the fireplace for a closer look? You may find yourself doing an about face!

While you were going for a spin, did you notice something out of the ordinary perched in the middle of the fireplace, on the opposite side? You'll have to retrieve this item. To do this, take in a little reading in the library. Pay particular attention to the first letter of each book's title. By pulling the books out in a certain order, you can create a word that will have a learned effect on your education.[10]

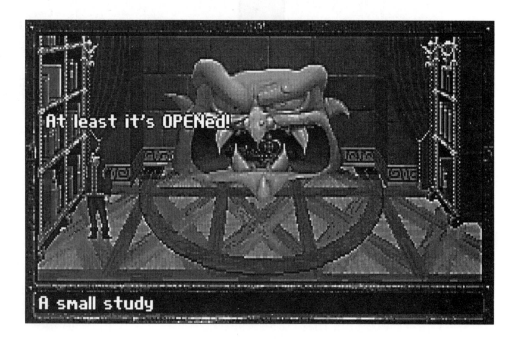

THE CATACOMBS

Have you figured out how to reach the catacombs?[11] It's dark here, but not so dark that wraiths live here. After a little wandering, you'll come across a magical force field. You must deactivate the force field in order to pass through it.[12]

A dank, dungeon passage

Once you're through it, you'll find two remaining rooms on either side. Inspect them closely and you'll find an item you need.[13] If it's too dark for you to see clearly, wait for your amulet to restore its power, then cast the will-o-wisp spell, to brighten things up a little.

UPSTAIRS

There are several bedrooms up here in which you'll find the stony prison sculptures of your dear friends Darm, Brynn, and Zanthia. Don't worry about trying to save them now. The only thing you need to find upstairs is a second key that unlocks the doors in the Great Hall. Hint: Finding the key requires solving a puzzle that's just waiting to be played.[14]

Gold key taken.

THE ROYAL FOYER

Beyond the Great Hall is the Royal Foyer.[15] Now is a good time to
save your game if you have not already, just in case things get messy
and you need to take another crack at finishing the game.

To the right, as you guessed, lies the Kyra-Vault. To open it, you
must solve the red-pillow puzzle lined up before you. Have you three
items to place on the pillows?[16] Experiment with the order of
placement until you achieve the right combination and the Kyra-Vault
opens.[17] But before you can take even a single step . . .

MALCOLM!

This time, he's ticked off. A little pushing and shoving will ensue. And
this time, charming Prince, you're ticked off, too. After all, he
destroyed your parents, didn't he? And he has had you running
around Kyrandia like a fool. And now this foolishness! This time,
Malcolm has pushed you too far.

Go ahead, give him a good wallop! Now, march right past him and
enter . . .

Royal Chalice taken.

THE KYRA-VAULT

But don't drop your guard for too long. In just a few seconds, Malcolm will follow you in. You'll have to work fast, or else Malcolm will cast a turn-to-stone spell on you, forever sealing your fate in concrete.

A quick look around and you see the enormous Kyragem in the center of the room, as well as a mirror on the right side. Think fast!

Hint: What goes around, comes around, as long as you're not standing in its way. But how do you trick Malcolm into thinking you're there one instant, gone the next? Perhaps taking a moment to reflect on a gift your mother gave you will do the trick?[18]

KYRANDIA IS SAVED!

After foiling Malcolm, Kallak is free of the stone shell which had contained him, and all of your friends are free again, too. The Lands weep no more, and Kyrandia is once again a peaceful place . . .

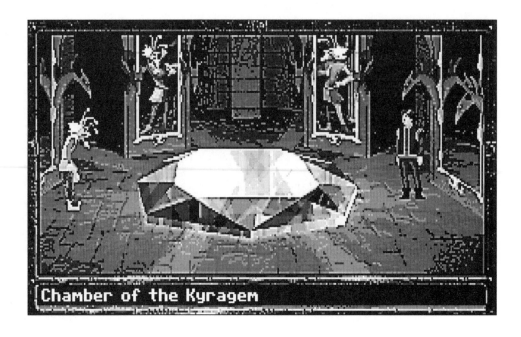

Chamber of the Kyragem

Chamber of the Kyragem

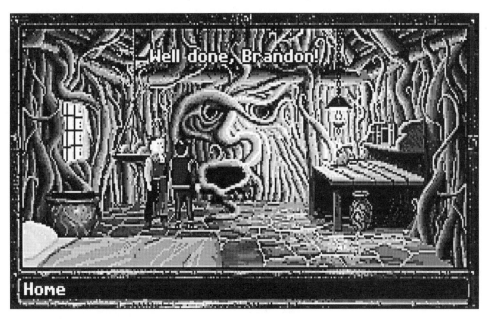

For a little while, anyway. Let's face it: We both know Malcolm won't sit tight very long. But don't worry, Prince Brandon, you've served your world well. So give yourself a hand, you've earned it.

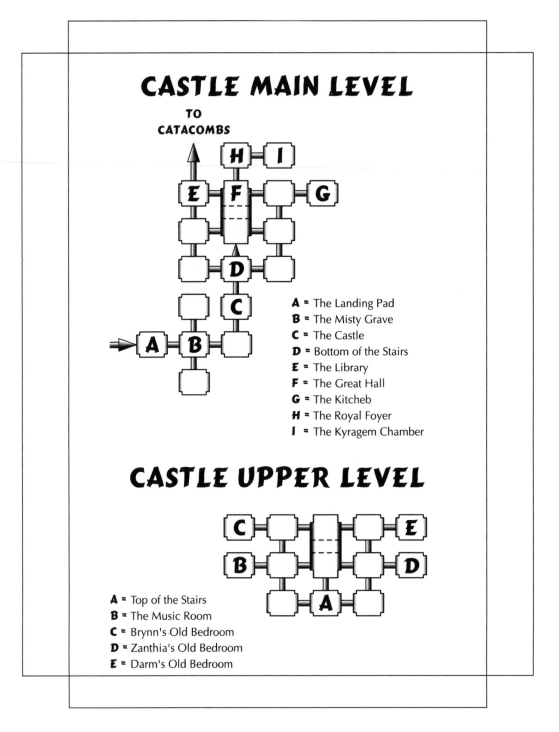

CASTLE MAIN LEVEL

TO
CATACOMBS

A = The Landing Pad
B = The Misty Grave
C = The Castle
D = Bottom of the Stairs
E = The Library
F = The Great Hall
G = The Kitcheb
H = The Royal Foyer
I = The Kyragem Chamber

CASTLE UPPER LEVEL

A = Top of the Stairs
B = The Music Room
C = Brynn's Old Bedroom
D = Zanthia's Old Bedroom
E = Darm's Old Bedroom

CASTLE CATACOMBS

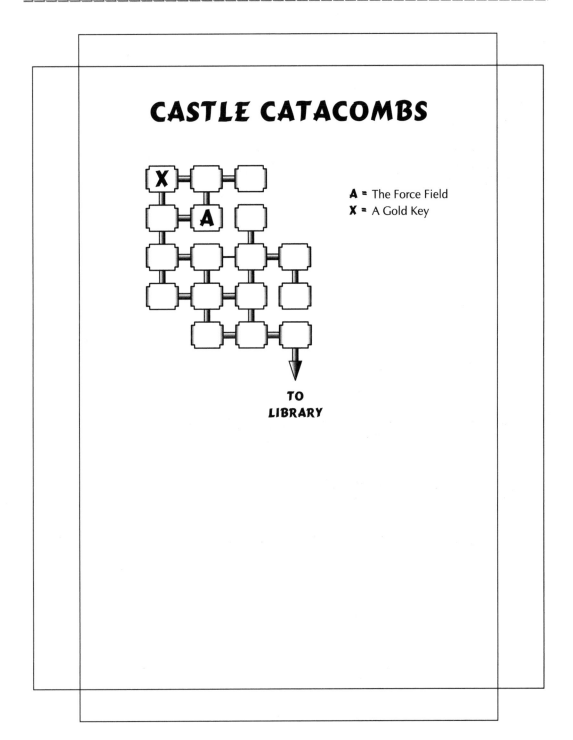

A = The Force Field
X = A Gold Key

TO
LIBRARY

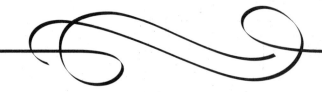

CLUENOTES

1 In this game, anyhow, but *h-e-e-e's b-a-a-a-ck* with a vengeance in Kyrandia 3!

2 The red orchid you brought with you. Lay it on the grave. (Actually, any flower will do.)

3 That's not the only item you'll need. You'll also need the Royal Sceptre, and the Royal Crown, which you'll find in the castle.

4 Here one minute, gone the next. This trick will come in handy when you don't want to be seen by others.

5 Here's where you use the Iron Key that you recovered from the room on the other side of the Volcanic River in Chapter 3.

6 Your mother's spirit will activate your amulet's red gem, which, when cast, makes you invisible for a short period of time. Use this to sneak up on the iron gate unnoticed by the gargoyles, open the lock, and go inside.

7 Don't get too close to Herman if you encounter him—he's under Malcolm's evil power now. You can use your yellow amulet gem to put him to sleep if you like, making it safe to skirt around him.

8 And since there are two doors, you'll need to find two keys, in order to get inside. Hint: One key is hidden in a secret area on the first level, and the second key is hidden upstairs in a secret place.

9 It's a Royal Sceptre, hanging beside a spoon above the table. It may or may not be disguised as a Mutton leg. If it is, click it once on the dirty countertop and it will change into the Sceptre. Then place it in your inventory.

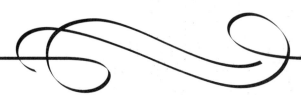

10 Pull out the books in the correct order to spell the word "OPEN," and the fireplace will spin around, revealing the hidden Crown, which you should take. If it doesn't seem to work, make sure that all of the other books are pushed in and that only the books whose first letter's spell "OPEN" are pulled out a little from their shelves. It won't work if any other books are pulled out.

11 The secret passage to the catacombs is in the Library. Step up to the fireplace to activate the secret passageway.

12 You remember what your blue amulet gem is good for, don't you? Hit it.

13 Search the floors very carefully. In the left room you'll see a stone out of place. Move it to uncover a gold key.

14 As in, the bells in the Music Room. Use the stick hanging on the side of the bell to strike out the correct four-note score. Hint: None of the notes are repeated, so that leaves only twelve combinations to try. The right order of notes to strike is: "Do-Fa-Mi-Re."

15 It takes two keys to open the locked doors in the Great Hall. The first one gets stuck, while the second one finishes the job and lets you in.

16 The three items you'll need are the Royal Chalice, the Royal Sceptre, which is hidden in the Kitchen, and the Royal Crown, which is hidden on the other side of the fireplace in the library.

17 The correct order is: Sceptre, Crown, Chalice.

18 As soon as Malcolm enters, stand in front of the mirror on the right side of the Kyra-Vault and then touch your red amulet gem to cast the invisibility spell.

BOOK 2

THE HAND OF FATE

CHAPTER 6

DARKMOOR SWAMP

Kyrandia is disappearing. Rock by rock, and tree by tree, Kyrandia ceases to exist. Royal Mystics are baffled. They have consulted every reference. They have even allowed Marko and his "*hand*some" new valet into the conference. Luckily, the Hand had experience in these matters and finally the Royal Mystics approved a plan, one that required retrieving a magic anchor stone from the Center of the World. They choose Zanthia, youngest of the Kyrandia mystics, to retrieve the stone.

THE TOSSED LAB

Okay, so you've got to save the world. If that's the way it's got to be, fine—but wait! Your lab has been turned upside-down by someone who obviously doesn't want you to succeed in your quest. The worst part is that the two most important tools of your trade, a cauldron and a spellbook, are missing. They are hidden nearby, outside your lab.[1]

Before you head outside, quickly search among the ruins of your lab to find three items of use.[2] After a quick change of clothes, it's time to go searching for your lost tools and whatever else you can find to help you on the long journey that lies ahead.[3]

GET THE GEAR

Your immediate surroundings have plenty to offer. At the Dock west of your house, a swamp tree vanishes as you approach. You can skip the mushroom growing here; it's of no use to you. To the west is a

Weed Patch. Don't get so distracted by those meat-eating flytrap plants that you miss the item hidden here.[4]

North of the Weed Patch you'll encounter the Gnarly Tree. Snap off one of its branches and add it to your inventory. There's an onion growing here, too. Take it as well. Also: West of the Ferry Station you'll come to a three-way Swamp Intersection. Notice the bird's nest?[5]

FERRY STATION

Ferry runner Brueth won't give you a ride to Morningmist Valley unless you've got gold to pay your fare. He suggests that you make some gold, since, after all, you are an alchemist! (Even after you find gold, things may not work out here as expected.[6])

QUICKSAND BOG

The crossing-the-quicksand puzzle here is a pushover.[7] With a little effort, you'll make your way across, retrieving the skeleton key on the way.

CROCODILE ROCK

The Crocodile is wagging his tail, but don't be fooled. He'll have you for lunch if you get too close. You don't want to completely ignore him, though. If you check your spellbook, you'll find that Lizard Tears are among the ingredients needed for potions. Now, if only you could make that crocodile spill a few tears of sadness. Or, for that matter, of joy—either way, they come out tears.[8]

There's also another item you can collect here—one of significant importance. A quick peek is all it takes to find it.[9]

HOT SULFUR SPRINGS

Pew! Hold your nose. Nothing smells worse than burning sulfur—except for rotten eggs, perhaps. Don't miss that Sulfur Rock sitting in the upper corner. It's a real stinker, which is exactly why you'll need it for one of your potions.[10] The steaming sulfur water here is also useful, but you'll need an empty flask to collect some.[11]

HERB'S: INSIDE AND OUT

Before you go inside Herb's Shack, pluck one of those fireberry clusters. You have to cool them down first.[12] Although Herb, inside the Shack, won't have any gold to give you, he does have a number of useful items you can take—a total of three, in fact.[13]

Herb's croaky little friends will suggest you dig up the Pirate's Treasure if it's gold you're looking for. That's good advice.[14] See the burning candle on Herb's desk? It could come in handy later if you need to heat some water.

THE FISHERMAN

These two guys are just trying to stay afloat. When you try to talk to them, they scold you for making too much noise. By the looks of it, they'll either sink or swim—and without any fish, since they haven't any bait. In your experience, cheese bait works best. Perhaps if you found some cheese[15] for them to use as bait, they would leave and you could use their boat to cross the sea. No, it doesn't look very sea-worthy, but perhaps there's a use for the boat other than crossing the sea.[16]

MARKO AND HIS HAND

At the Cave Entrance you'll meet Marko and his helpful Hand. Marko is shocked to hear that your Lab has been tossed. He asks if he can help you, but he doesn't have any gold, nor does he know what's inside the cave he just emerged from. The fact is, it's Marko who will need your help a little later, if you feel like giving him a helping hand.[17] We'll deal with Marco later. Before you go in the cave, it's a good idea to head one screen south first, to . . .

THE FIREFLY TREE

Touch these buzzers and they'll make music and teach you a tune you'll need a little later.[18] The trick here is to play "Simon-Says" and follow along as prompted by the lead fly. To do this, click on any one of the fireflies to find out the first note of the tune. If the firefly plays the note twice, followed by another note, then that is the first firefly note in the tune. If, however, the first firefly you touch plays only one note, then another firefly plays a note, it is the second firefly that actually starts the tune. Touch it, and it will play the note again, followed by a second firefly, playing its own note. Touch the flies again to repeat the notes in sequence, and a third firefly will play a note . . . and so on, until the entire tune is completed (and the fireflies go into a sort of jamming, mini-meltdown for a few bars).

Write down the order of the notes and the color of each firefly as they play them, so you remember this later, as you will need it.[19] For example, you might write: Red, Purple, Blue, Green, Yellow, Aqua, Orange.

There is an easier way to get the fireflies to play the tune for you: Give them something to eat.[20]

TWISTY TUNNEL AND RAT FACE

The snoozing Rat here has no intention of letting you pass. You're going to have to pull a little magic to get by him. Finally, you get to flex your Alchemist muscle and have a little fun. Let's see, serving up a good scare will probably do the trick.[21]

Hot water you collect will cool quickly if you don't use it right away. You can go back to the Sulfur Spring to collect more and concoct your potion there, or go to Herb's place, heat up a bottle of water over his candle, and use that to make the potion.

THE SKULL CAVE

It's too dark to enter this room unless you have a fireberry in your inventory.[22] Remember that little tune the fireflies taught you? Here's where it comes into play. Test each of the skull's teeth to see the color each one represents, then repeat the firefly tune in the same color order that they taught you. When the mouth drops open, use the special key[23] you found to open the chest inside and retrieve the fabulous prizes inside.[24] It's that simple.

THE (DOLTISH) DRAGONFLY

All that work to find some gold to pay for a ferry trip and then—poof, no more ferry! The well-meaning but nonetheless dim-witted Dragonfly who delivers mail in these parts has accidentally sneezed flames on the boat and turned it to cinders!

He says he'll personally take you to Morningmist Valley, if you can find the four letters he lost. They're scattered in all directions, and finding them isn't too difficult—they're lying in plain view at locations you've been to already.[25] Once you've found them and returned them to the Dragonfly, he'll give you a ride to Morningmist Valley.

For fun, though not necessarily to complete your quest, can you figure out a way to open the letters and read them before you return them to the Dragonfly?[26]

Don't worry about gathering ingredients for potions to take with you to Morningmist Valley. When you land, you'll find out why they won't make a difference.

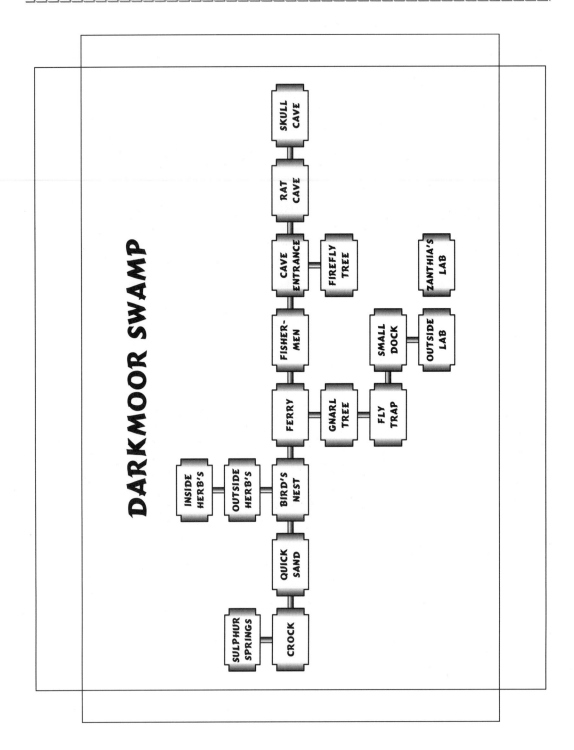

CLUENOTES

1 Go ahead and stretch your legs a little. Get to know these parts—chances are you'll find the first few items you need on your own. If you don't, more clues are up ahead.

2 A flask of water, hidden beneath the rumpled rug; an empty flask on the bottom shelf of the bookcase; and some blueberries.

3 Don't miss those blueberries right outside your door. While you're at it, give those lurking swamp eyes a poke. Unlike Brandon with his troubles in Kyrandia 1, you're a little tougher when it comes to beasties.

4 It's your spellbook, and it's hidden inside the hollow tree trunk. Unfortunately, it's missing quite a few pages. Still, a thin spellbook is better than no spellbook.

5 It doesn't contain a golden egg; however there is a feather inside. Take it, for it just might tickle the fancy of an otherwise humorless beast.

6 A friendly but clumsy Dragonfly will accidentally do serious damage to the ferry. Fortunately, he'll offer you a way to Morningmist Valley, but you'll have to help him before he'll help you.

7 Give the tree a little shove and *Voilà*, you've created a bridge.

8 Feed him either of the onions you find (one near Gnarly Tree, the other at the Cave Entrance), or tickle him with the feather you snatched from the bird's nest at the three-way Swamp Intersection.

9 Look inside the tree hole and you'll find your cauldron.

10 It makes the perfect, no-cholesterol substitute for the smell of (rotten) eggs.

11 There's another flask at Herb's Shack. He'll let you take it if you ask him. The sulfur water, if used immediately after collecting it in a flask, will work as hot water for potions that require hot water.

12 With water, of course. Any water will do: swamp water, clear water . . . any water.

13 A bag of manure (which is really plant food—know any hungry plants?), a toad stool (the little red, unoccupied one), and a flask.

14 There is a treasure chest in Skull Cave. However, it doesn't contain gold. It has some items that will help you another way, though.

15 Which you'll find in the Skull Cave. To get it, you'll need to scare away the Rat guard. You'll need a fireberry to light the way into the Skull Cave, and you'll need to learn a tune from the fireflies in order to pick the toothy skull head lock. Once that's open, you'll need a special key to open the treasure chest.

16 The fishermen promise to give you their lead anchor after they catch a fish. They catch a fish, but then they vanish! Don't panic—their boat, with the anchor in it, is docked just north of your lab. Use your newly acquired alchemist's magnet, located in the Skull Cave, to turn the anchor from lead into gold. Finally!

17 Actually, since his own helping Hand is nowhere to be found, you can release him by feed the plant holding him hostage some plant food, which can be found at Herb's Shack.

18 To open the skull in the cave beyond the Twisted Tunnel, which you can enter once you scare off the Rat guarding the entrance.

19 The firefly tune changes each time you replay Hand of Fate, so pay close attention to the order of notes and the color each note corresponds with.

20 No, not fireberries. But you're on the right track. Just pretend they're fruit flies and serve them accordingly.

21 Create the Swampsnake Potion, then let Rat Face have it. Or, for a real hair-raising experience, drink it yourself. If you followed the clues that have come before this, you'll have everything you need (the little Toad Stool, Lizard Tears from the Crocodile, Onion, the rotten-egg smelling sulfur stone, and Windy Woof, which is also known as Gnarlybark—as in, Bark = Woof, Woof, get it?) The only thing you may need to get again is hot water.

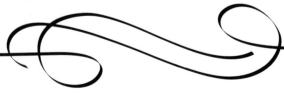

22 You can get one outside Herb's Shack, at the fireberry bush. Pour water on one of the glowing berries to cool it off, then pick it off the bush and put it in your inventory.

23 The Skull Key, which can be found in the middle of the quicksand pit. If you don't have the key, topple over the tree by the quicksand pit to create a bridge, then walk across and snatch the key.

24 The first is the alchemist magnet, which, besides letting you turn gold to lead and lead to gold, you can use on people to find out their true feelings or motivations—in other words, what's really going on inside their head—despite what they may say to your face. (Case in point: When Marko winds up upside down, try the alchemist magnet on him and see what he says!) The second item is a chunk of moldy cheese, which you can give to the fisherman to use as bait.

25 A letter can be found at the roof of your house, at the Quicksand Bog, at the Firefly Tree, and at the Sulfur Springs.

26 Hold them over the rising steam at the Sulfur Springs to open them.

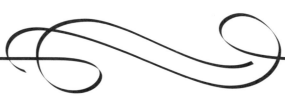

CHAPTER 7

MORNINGMIST VALLEY

Thank goodness there's a haystack to fall in after Firefly drops you off here in Morningmist Valley. Unfortunately, somewhere between Darkmoor Swamp and the Valley, you lost all of your items. Don't worry, the items you'll need for this part of your quest, including your Alchemist Magnet, are scattered around nearby.[1] Morningmist Valley is a rather small place. To the east is a large guarded gate, which is where you really need to go. But getting through will prove challenging, and you'll have to figure out a way to

tempt the guards to open the gate and let you enter. By combing Morningmist Valley and enlisting the support of others, you'll find everything you need to solve the gate puzzle.

THE HAYSTACK

When you land here you'll discover that your items are missing. Look around and see what you can recover and what new items are here.[2] Pick up the letter—it's addressed to someone nearby.[3]

If you leave the Haystack and come back later, you'll encounter new creatures. Before you bother with the sheep, talk to the ghost and do what he tells you.[4]

Meanwhile, head west to the gate into Highmoon City and see what you can find out from those unyielding guards.

CITY GATE

Forget trying the nice approach to convince the guards to let you in. It's going to take some coaxing to change their minds about you. They'll throw you a number of lines about rules and regulations regarding the gate, but you can ignore these red herrings. Befriending the guards is your only option. But how?[5] Perhaps if you had something to offer them.[6]

FARMER GREENBERRY

At first, this guy isn't much help. But if you give him something that's addressed to him, he'll come around.[7] He'll share his family's recipe for mustard, which is to mix vinegar with ground radish. You'll need the mustard to make sandwiches. The vinegar is right here, and Farmer Greenberry won't mind if you take it. The radishes, however, aren't as readily available.[8]

As for the sleeping dragon, he's just a pup. It's okay to pet him. Try to take his bowl and he'll carry on like a baby.[9]

You'll need to get into the farmer's basement, but he won't let you in no matter how much you beg. If only you could make him get off his duff and go away so you could slip into the basement. Hint: Take care of the ghost's request first, and the farmer won't be a problem anymore.

A BRIEF INTERMISSION

At some point during your travels in Morningmist Valley, the game will cut to a brief scene in which Marko scolds his helping Hand. It seems the Hand has been caught with your stolen stirring paddle. Rather suspicious, isn't it?

THE GARDEN

Aha! Your Alchemist Magnet. Take it. Remember, this tool is handy for getting people to tell the truth.[10] The garden contains mere sprouts, much too small to pick. If they were larger, they would be useful, but the big elephant hose seems stuck. You'll have to repair it in order to water the garden.[11] Once you water the garden, it will sprout two vegetables—radishes[12] and heads of lettuce—which you'll need to make the sandwiches.

There's a scarecrow in the middle of the garden, just hanging around bothering no*body*. Get the hint?[13]

THE CELLAR

Once the farmer leaves his seat, you can enter his Cellar by way of the double storm doors on the side of his house. Inside, you'll find a pair of shears,[14] four old horseshoes, and an Acme Cheesemaker. With the right ingredient, you can make cheese,[15] which is one of the ingredients you'll need to make sandwiches.

THE WATER WHEEL

Notice the pipes attached to the Water Wheel? They lead to the Garden. The Wheel is stuck, but by unjamming it, you'll get it turning again.[16] Hint: Once it's working, you'll need to turn the wheel on the pipe to get the water running again.

The Water Wheel also operates the huge, pounding hand grinder. In order to make sandwiches, you'll need some ground wheat. Have you found the wheat yet?[17] To collect the wheat you'll need a bowl.[18]

Be careful not to get too close the sparking axle—it could have a devastating effect on your life.[19]

MAKING SANDWICHES

Clues are scattered throughout the above topics to help you figure out how to make sandwiches. If you're still stuck on this puzzle, however, skip to this cluenote[20] for the complete solution.

BEFORE YOU LEAVE

Have you figured out what those shears are for? Use them to clip some wool from the sheep and take the wool. Also: Get some Lizard Tears by giving the dragon his bowl and taking it away again, collecting the spilled tears in your flask. You should also have the four horseshoes[21] that you found in the Farmer's cellar. With these items on hand, you're ready to go back to the gate and tempt the guards away from their post with the sandwich. You may now enter the town of Highmoon.

Faun Home: After walking through the gate, turn around and walk back out, and you'll make a telepathic, long-distance call to Faun back home.

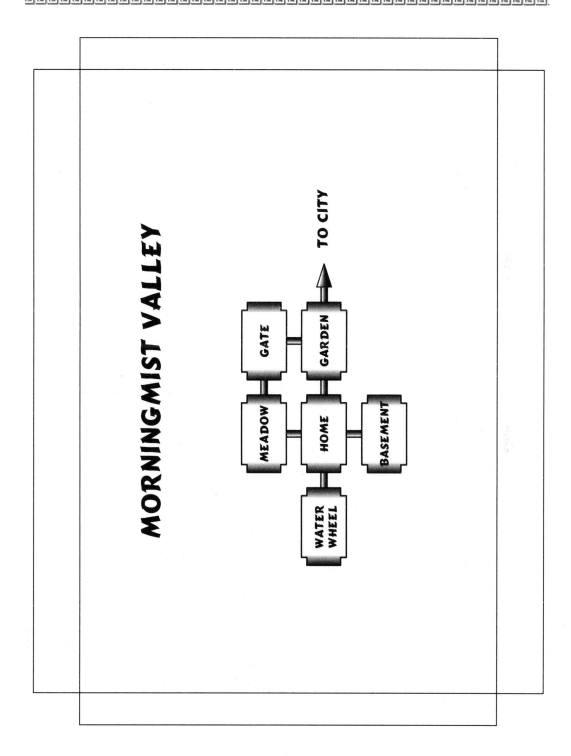

CLUENOTES

1 It's located in the Farmer's Garden.

2 Ever heard the saying, "Like trying to find a needle in a haystack?" Go ahead and have a look. You'll come out with an empty flask. Also: Pluck the two strands of wheat growing in the field on either side of the haystack.

3 If you managed to steam the letter open in the last chapter, you'll recall that the letter is addressed to Farmer Greenberry. Give it to him, and he'll give you a clue that will help you get past the guards.

4 The ghost won't appear until you've talked to the guards at the gate. Collect the ghost into the empty flask you found in the haystack. The ghost claims that if you get him a big body he'll beat up the guards. However that isn't *really* how you're going to change the guards' collective mind. And no, the ghost won't be interested in occupying the Farmer's body — there's another body the ghost wants, one that's even less animated that the Farmer's.

5 Have you found your Alchemist Magnet? It's lying in the Garden, nearby. Remember, you can use it to get others to tell the truth. In this case, use the magnet on the guards and you'll find out what they love.

6 Their weakness is sandwiches, which you'll have to make yourself. The recipe is in your spellbook. All of the ingredients can be gathered here in Morningmist Valley.

7 Give him the letter.

8 Have you visited the Garden yet? No, there aren't any radishes or heads of lettuce growing here, but perhaps with a little watering you could get them to grow.

9 Which is fine, since you're going to need both the bowl and some dragon tears.

10 The farmer will flat out tell you that he's not leaving his seat unless the scarecrow (in the garden) runs past him. How do you make a scarecrow run? The ghost can help you.

11 Go fix the Water Wheel.

12 Actually, you'll use the radish with the vinegar to make mustard. You'll need to grind the radish first at the Water Wheel grinder. Collect the ground radish in the baby dragon's bowl, then pour vinegar on the bowl to make mustard.

13 Pour the ghost on the Scarecrow. He'll take off and will have a helpful effect on the heretofore lazy Farmer, who'll chase after the Scarecrow. Now you can go into the basement.

14 These will come in handy for a little wool-gathering.

15 Milk, which you can collect in your flask from the sheep. Pour the milk into the funnel atop the cheesemaker, pull the lever, and out will pop a chunk of cheese.

16 Remove the stick that's stuck in the wheel by the top of the steps.

17 There are two stalks of wheat near the haystack, where you started.

18 Take the baby dragon's bowl from in front of the farmhouse.

19 Actually, it will kill you, so don't touch it. But there is something you can touch to it to create a new item. You will use the new item later in the game. See the very last cluenote in this chapter for more information.

20 You'll need ground wheat, mustard, lettuce, and cheese. Make the mustard first by grinding the radish in the Water Wheel grinder, and retrieving it in the dragon's bowl. Pour the vinegar on the ground radish in the bowl, and you'll have mustard. Pour the mustard into your cauldron, and add a head of lettuce from the garden and the chunk of cheese you made in the Farmer's cellar. Finally, grind a stalk of wheat (that you took from the field by the haystack) in the grinder, retrieve the ground wheat in the dragon's bowl, and pour it in the cauldron with the other ingredients. An orange potion will appear. Collect it in your empty vial, then give the vial to yourself to create a sandwich. Now you can tempt the guards with the sandwich and through the gate.

21 If you want to save yourself a lot of time in the next chapter, click on the horseshoes to find out which ones you "have a funny feeling about." Take one that you *don't* have a funny feeling about and touch it to the electric spark at the Waterwheel. The horseshoe will turn into a magnet, which you'll need later.

CHAPTER 8

HIGHMOON VILLAGE

Get ready for a lot of running around, Zanthia. Highmoon is a rather large place, and there's much work to be done here. Your instincts are correct: You've got to find a boat to take you to Volcania. By wandering around, you will find some objects to take—for starters, that long stick plugging the Seahorse Fountain's mouth.

At the street east of the town entrance, you'll find four items lying on the ground. One of them is a missing page from your spellbook. Take the page and click it on your spellbook to bind it where it Belongs. Opening your spellbook reveals two new potions: The Teddy Bear Potion and the Skeptic Spell. The spellbook clearly states that the Skeptic Spell, for which you have some of the required ingredients, must be activated on the Altar of Doubt.

THE DRUNKEN DRAGON TAVERN

Have you noticed that everyone seems to be walking around in a trance or sleeping? Weird stuff. However, it seems that some of the town's residents were spared the trauma. You'll find them in the Tavern north of the town's gate. Getting inside the tavern will require playing the same musical combination that you played earlier in the Skull Cave, except instead of hitting teeth, you'll hit those buttons to the left of the door. Do you remember the tune? If not, you can pick the Tavern's lock, using a dull but serviceable tool you found a little earlier.[1]

Inside, the crowd looks more threatening then they really are.[2] Look around, and you'll find something useful hidden in here.[3] Help yourself to a mug of root beer and put it in your inventory.

By talking to the pirates, you'll find out that the mustard barge is the only ship that goes close to Volcania. They warn you, however, that no one goes to Volcania because it's too dangerous. Like that's going to stop you? What will stop you, however, is the parrot by the door. No one leaves the Tavern until he or she recites a poem.[4]

After you leave, make sure you come back again later. There will be a brawl in progress, begun over the literary merits, or lack thereof, of your recital. Hang around for a few moments and one of the pirates will lose something valuable that you can take,[5] but you'll have to perform a little magic to get it.[6]

THE GAMBLING OCTOPUS

When you leave the tavern you'll find a gambling octopus waiting for you outside. He invites you to play a shell game. There's a sucker born every minute, and you'll wind up proving that theory—unless, that is, you've got a lucky charm to put down along with the gold wager[7] the octopus demands. Have you any lucky items on hand?[8]

If you accidentally gamble away your only gold, go back to the tavern and witness another brawl—you'll be equally rewarded, as above.

THE ALTAR OF DOUBT

On your way to the Altar of Doubt, you'll climb a hill that leads to a gorge. At the foot of the hill there's a huge statue of a rabbit with one paw raised. Since the Skeptic Spell requires a Rabbit Footprint, now is as good a time as any to get one. Next to the rabbit is a mud puddle. You can get the rabbit's footprint with the mud.[9]

At the top of the hill is the Gorge you must cross to reach the Altar of Doubt. Let's see, there's a rope here. And it looks long enough to swing across to the other side. However, a leap for the rope won't work.[10] Do you have something in your inventory that will allow you to hook the rope and bring it closer, so you can grab it?[11]

Once you reach the Altar of Doubt, you must place the Skeptic Spell serum on the platform to activate it. You should have all of the items[12] that you'll need, except for Sweet and Sour sauce, which you'll have to make. Hint: Mix the sweet and sour sauce in the Baby Dragon's bowl. To make the sauce, you'll need something sweet, like candy or a soft drink, and something sour, like citrus or vinegar.[13]

Once you've got Sweet and Sour sauce, mix it with the other ingredients in your cauldron to complete the Skeptic Spell serum. Fill *two* vials with the purple serum, then place each, one at a time, on the altar, to create the complete the Skeptic Spell potion. The potion can actually fill four vials, but since you only have two vials, you'll have to come back later to turn another vial of the serum into a potion.[14]

SERVING JAIL TIME

Between the street and the hill that leads to the Altar of Doubt there lies the town jail. You can't get inside, though, as the sheriff, in some sort of trance, is blocking the doorway. A certain spell that you recently added to your book will free his mind and remove him from the doorway.[15]

Inside, Marko is up to his ears in trouble again, this time behind bars. Freeing him is optional. You don't have to help him if you don't want to. If you do, though, you'll need the key that's outside in the water, beneath the jail. Marko suggests you use a magnet to get the key; however he isn't referring to your Alchemist Magnet.[16]

Once you have the key and have attempted to free Marko, you'll wind up in trouble yourself. If you try to free yourself using the magnet, the sheriff will put you back in the slammer and throw the key out the window, where a fish swallows it. To get it back, use something in the jail cell to create a fishing line.[17]

THE STOREKEEPER

Like the sheriff, the storekeeper is zonked out, under the power of some sort of spell. You'll need his help, for, according to the pirates at the Tavern, the storekeeper can sell you passage to Mustard Island, which is as close to Volcania as anyone dares sail. To wake the storekeeper, you'll need the Skeptic Spell[18], which is described in your spellbook.[19] (While you're here, take a moment to study the map on the wall.)

Once you bring the storekeeper back to the land of the living, he'll tell you that a ticket to Mustard Island costs three gold coins. He won't accept gold teeth in place of gold coins. You'll have to change the gold teeth into gold coins. Hint: "Hand pressing" them will do the trick.[20]

THE WHARF

Once you've purchased a voucher from the Storekeeper, you can proceed to the Wharf and set sail for Mustard Island. The ship's captain will be under the influence of the same zombie spell that afflicted the storekeeper and the sheriff, so you'll need to serve him some of the Skeptic Spell potion as well.[21]

Before you give the Captain your voucher, make sure you save your game. Then, hand over your ticket, and the Captain will let you on board and will set sail for . . .

MUSTARD ISLAND

This is a dangerous place, and no good comes from landing here. No matter what you do, the Cannibals will eat you. Actually, you don't even want to come here at all—it's Volcania you're trying to get to, remember?

HOW NOT TO GET EATEN
BY CANNIBALS

Once you set sail, you'll need to change the ship's course. If you don't, you'll end up on Mustard Island, where you'll be eaten by Cannibals. (You can offer them a sandwich, but eventually they'll eat you anyway, so don't even bother with the finger food—so to speak.)

Where you really want to go is Volcania, which, according to the map you saw earlier at the shopkeeper's, lies just north of Mustard

Island. To avoid Mustard Island, you'll need to change the ship's course once it sets sail. Changing course requires some "excess force" on the ship's compass but no exertion on your part—just an item in your inventory that has a lot of "pull."[22]

Because you diverted the ship's course, the Captain will be so angry with you that he will toss you overboard. Don't panic—you're a good swimmer, and Volcania is only a short swim away. Stroke!

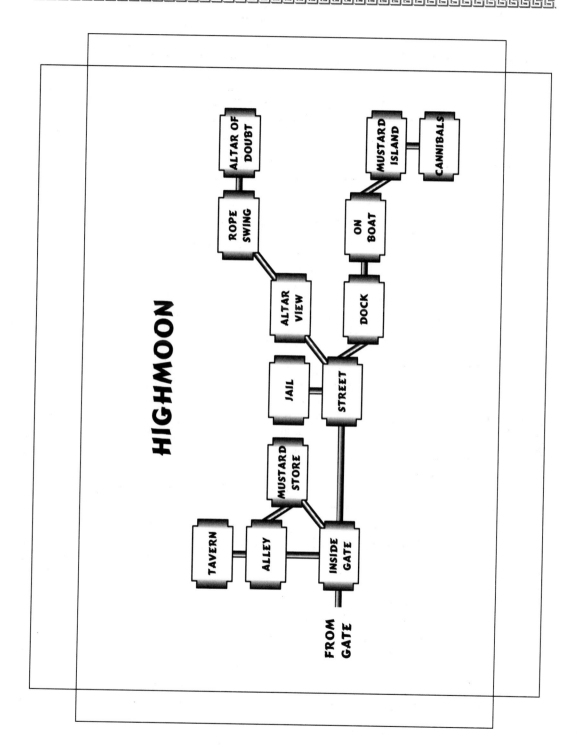

HIGHMOON

CLUENOTES

1 Pick the lock with the scissors you snatched from the Farmer's cellar.

2 For fun, try using your Alchemist's Magnet on each one to hear what they're really thinking.

3 Taffy, hidden in the barrel in the corner.

4 Click on the podium to start reciting your poem.

5 A gold tooth, which you can use in a game of chance.

6 The pirate won't let you have his gold tooth, for it is valuable. But if you turn it into lead while it's on the ground, he won't mind at all if you snatch it. Outside the Tavern, use your magnet on the lead tooth to turn it back into gold.

7 You'll need gold to play the game, and the only gold you'll find is a gold pirate tooth inside the Drunken Dragon Tavern, during the brawl.

8 The horseshoes you snatched from the Farmer's cellar earlier. Some are good luck, some not. To find out which will guarantee you a winner at the shell game, try each horseshoe on yourself. If it's a lucky one, lay it on the ground, *then* play the octopus' game. Hint: The one's you have a funny feeling about are the lucky ones. He'll only let you win twice, which is fine, for that will leave you with three pieces of gold.

9 Take some mud and click it on the rabbit's foot. You can also use taffy to get the impression if you prefer—it's hidden in the barrel in the Tavern.

10 Talk about a real cliffhanger of an ending!

11 You can reach the rope with the long stick, which you took from the Seahorse Fountain's mouth.

12 For the Lizard Tears, you should still have a vial containing the Dragon Tears from the baby Dragon back at the Farmer's place. A lucky horseshoe is one that you have "a funny feeling about" when you click it on yourself. And the rabbit's footprint you picked up before climbing the gorge hill, by touching some of the mud nearby on the rabbit's foot.

13 You can get root beer in the Tavern and Taffy in the barrel in the Tavern. On the street, you'll find an orange peel, and you already have vinegar from Farmer Greenberry.

14 You'll use a potion each on: the sheriff, the storekeeper, and the ship captain.

15 Use the Skeptic Spell on him, to bring him back to his senses.

16 Okay, here's the total solution to this puzzle, since it's probably impossible to figure out otherwise. Take one of the unlucky horseshoes back to the Waterwheel in Morningmist Valley and *carefully* magnetize it by touching it to the electrical spark created by the Waterwheel's axle.

17 Pulling apart the bedding will reveal some thread, to which Marko will attach a hook. Use the line and hook to catch the fish by clicking on the window. After you free yourself, you can free Marko by unlocking the right-hand lock.

18 Refer to "The Altar of Doubt," above, for clues on creating the Skeptic Spell.

19 If, that is, you found the missing spellbook page on the street outside the jail.

20 Remember the giant hand grinder at the Waterwheel? Place each gold tooth in the grinder to stamp them into gold coins.

21 Since you only had two vials to hold the Skeptic Spell potion, you'll have to go back to the Altar of Doubt with another vial of serum and create a third potion.

22 The horseshoe magnet. Drop it in the coil of rope beside the ship's wheel *as soon as you set sail*, and it will sway the ship's "auto-pilot" compass off the Mustard Island course and toward Volcania.

CHAPTER 9

VOLCANIA AND THE CENTER OF THE WORLD

Finally, you've made it to Volcania! Unfortunately you'll wash ashore with nothing in your knapsack except your Alchemist's Magnet, which is especially handy when used on the people you meet here to learn tips on what you need to do. Remember: Your

goal is to get to the Center of the World. For starters, pick up the starfish lying here.

HOT-FOOTING AND BEACH-COMBING ACROSS VOLCANIA

The most dangerous thing about Volcania is its terrain. Be careful not to step in any of the hot lava pools, or else you'll burn, baby. There *is* a safer way to travel around the island, which you'll discover by checking your spellbook.[1] You don't have to make this spell, however—simply watching your step and treading carefully will prevent any hot-lava mishaps.

Make sure you don't drop any useful items in or close to lava pools, as they will burn up and be gone forever.

Near the beach where you arrived, that ever-present (and always useful) long stick will turn up. Take it. You'll also find two heavy rocks on the island, which you should take, as you will need them later.

SALESMEN— OR, WHEN OPPORTUNITY KNOCKS, HALF LISTEN

All of the salesmen you meet will try to sell you items in exchange for seashells or sand dollars. You can ignore the salesman, the seashells, and the sand dollars, since none of the objects they offer you is useful. Except for one salesman, that is, who offers to sell you a red leather brochure in exchange for two starfish.[2]

A NICE SALES COUPLE— SORT OF

You'll meet an elderly sales team who gives you a promotional quill pen, free of charge. It will come in handy for a spell you may create for zooming around Volcania more safely.[3] They'll also try to sell you a map, but don't bother shelling over any loot for it because you won't need it.[4] Take the empty flask[5] and heavy rock here.

FLYING SHOES POTION

Creating this potion isn't necessary for your quest.[6] When you apply the potion to yourself it will create a pair of slick red shoes. Click them on yourself to wear them. While you are wearing the shoes, a shoehorn will appear in your inventory. Click it on yourself to remove the Flying Red Shoes.

Important Tip: If you decide to use the Flying Shoes, make sure you don't accidentally lose the shoehorn or burn it in one of the lava pits.[7]

JESSICA FROM MILTONIA

While wandering, you'll encounter Jessica, an apprentice from Miltonia. She doesn't have much to say and is of no assistance to you or your quest.[8]

THE CENTER OF THE WORLD

To get to the center of the world, you'll need the two heavy rocks you found lying around the island.[9] By carrying them in your inventory, you'll be heavy enough to drop down one of the two large steaming vents on the island.[10] Go ahead and take the plunge!

If you're wearing your Flying Red Shoes, you won't be able to drop down the vent until you remove them.

When you hit bottom, you'll wind up almost completely empty-handed again. Since your red dress didn't hold up well on the ride down,[11] you'll pull off another quick wardrobe change. Look around and you'll see a number of useful items.[12]

DINO TROUBLES

To get to the Anchor Stone room, which lies beyond the horny-nosed Triceratops, you'll need to get the three dinosaurs here to cooperate with you. Clicking on each dinosaur gives you a clue as to how to deal with it.

THE STEGOSAURUS

In the room with the Stegosaurus, you'll see sparkling pebbles attached the ceiling. You'll need to get these. Watch long enough, and you'll notice that the Stegosaurus acts like a dog that wants to play fetch. Have you found your trusty stick yet?[13] Toss the stick to the Stegosaurus and he'll retrieve it. After the second toss, he'll cause a rumble that will make some rocks fall and plug up a nearby steam vent, which in turn causes the vent beneath the sparkling pebbles to stream upward with great force. Stand in the vent and you'll be jetted in the air to the pebbles, coming down with two.[14]

T-REX

If you listen carefully during your Stegosaurus visit, Zanthia will think aloud about her idea to create a teddy bear for bait. A little bare-back riding is in order for the T-Rex, but you'll need something to steer him with. Hence, the Teddy Bear. You'll need fuzz, a heart of gold, and two pebbles. The heart is easy to find—just look for a lump of lead shaped like a heart and change it into gold.[15] As for the pebbles, you can get those by dealing with the Stegosaurus. The last item, fuzz, is practically right under your nose in T-Rex's room. Hint: While money doesn't grow on trees, fuzz does.[16] Make sure you have both the stick and the Teddy Bear in your inventory, then go ahead and leap on T-Rex's back. After a wild ride, you'll wind up with an item[17] that you can now use to trick the Triceratops.

TRICERATOPS

Once again, your powers of deduction prove correct. You need to get the Triceratops to crash through the Anchor Stone door so you can get inside. The item you collected while riding on T-Rex's back will come in handy for tricking the Triceratops into storming the door.[18]

Before you pull this one off, however, make sure the Triceratops is facing the right way or else he'll charge you rather than the door.[19] *Olé!*

THE ANCHOR STONE ROOM

At last, the Anchor Stone. Actually, stones. There are several of them here, but before you can do anything, Jessica makes an appearance, as does Marko. Marko updates you on what's gone down in Kyrandia. He says that the real problem has nothing to do with the foolish Anchor stones, and that you've got to get up to the Wheel of Fate, which, for some reason, is causing everything to vanish. But before Marko can whisk you through the portal, his suspicious helping Hand snatches him away, and Jessica follows.

A quick call to Faun reveals that the Kyrandia Wheels, which reside high in the clouds and beyond the Enchanted Forest, are stuck or something, and that you better fix them. Fast.

Before you leave, make sure you pick up the spell page lying here and click it on your spellbook to bind it inside. (You don't need to take an Anchor Stone.)

LEAVING VOLCANIA

Remember that little vent trick that helped you get the two pebbles?
The same idea works to jet you up and out of Volcania. You need to
be in the Triceratops room. Notice that little platform floating in the
middle of the circular lava pool? It works like an elevator, but only if
you can create a lava eruption by causing a steam build-up. Hint:
Have you found those heavy rocks?[20]

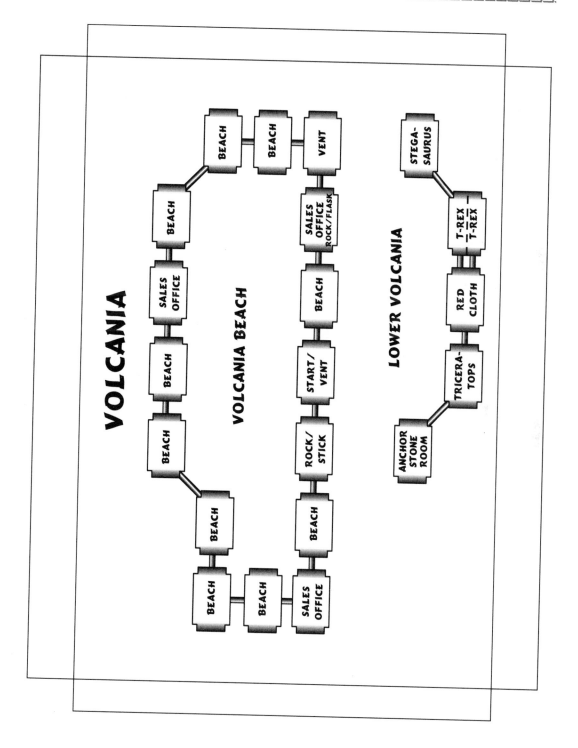

VOLCANIA

VOLCANIA BEACH

BEACH

BEACH

VENT

BEACH

SALES OFFICE

BEACH

BEACH

BEACH

BEACH

BEACH

SALES OFFICE

SALES OFFICE ROCK/FLASK

BEACH

START/ VENT

ROCK/ STICK

BEACH

LOWER VOLCANIA

STEGA-SAURUS

T-REX / T-REX

RED CLOTH

TRICERA-TOPS

ANCHOR STONE ROOM

CLUENOTES

1 Flying Shoes Potion.

2 Two starfish will buy you a promotional folio from the salesman seated at a desk outside a cave entrance. The portfolio is made of red leather, which is one of the required ingredients for making Flying Shoes Potion.

3 The promotional quill pen is actually a Feather of Snipe, which is one of the ingredients you'll need to concoct the Flying Shoes Potion, if you decide you want to bother with it.

4 Do try your Alchemist's Magnet on the woman. She'll give you an important clue on how to get to the Center of the World.

5 Use the vial to collect hot air from any one of the steaming vents. Hot air is one of the ingredients you'll need to create Flying Shoes Potion, if you decide you want to make this potion. It isn't necessary for completing this chapter.

6 The ingredients: the old woman behind the desk will give you a quill pen, which is really a Feather of Snipe; the salesman outside the cave will sell you a leather brochure for two starfish; you can obtain a flask near the old woman to capture hot air from one of the island's many steaming vents. Mix all these ingredients together in your cauldron, and you'll have the Flying Shoes potion.

7 Without the shoehorn, you can't remove your Flying Shoes, which makes it impossible for your to fall down one of the vents to the Center of the World.

8 Though using your Alchemist's Magnet on her yields humorous results.

9 One is west of where you arrived, the other beside the old woman behind the desk.

10 There's one on the beach where you arrived, and another to the right of the old man and old woman sales team.

11 Notice there's still a piece of it stuck at the vent hole entrance, in the upper left corner. You'll need to recover it, but not just yet. We'll come back to it in a few shakes.

12 There are only a few screens in this area, so finding items takes only a little roaming. You'll find two lumps of lead. One of them is more useful than the other. You'll need to change one of them into gold. Hint: Have you noticed one is shaped like a heart? You'll also find four heavy rocks in your wanderings—take them as well.

13 It's lying on the ground to the right of the lava cavern entrance, in Mr. T-Rex's room.

14 Which you'll need to create the Teddy Bear.

15 There are two lumps of lead lying around, so make sure you find the one that looks like a heart.

16 Gather some fuzz from the short palm tree beneath the platform.

17 It's a piece of your red dress.

18 Ever seen a bullfight? Yes, they're pretty high up there on the list of mankind's worst ills. But thankfully you won't be harming this creature. Use the piece of red dress for the same purpose.

19 Each time you leave the Triceratops and come back, he'll be facing a different direction. Wait for him to face the door, then do your red dress trick on him.

20 Place the rocks over the steaming vent spouts throughout the underground realm to plug them up and cause a steam build-up. The locations are the Stegosaurus room (beside the emerald stairs), the Chamber of the Anchor, the Triceratops room, and near the Emerald Bridge.

CHAPTER 10

THE ENCHANTED FOREST

What a blast! You're getting closer to your eventual fate, but you're not there yet. Luckily, the Enchanted Forest is very small. Getting through it will take some puzzling. As usual, you've landed with almost no items.

THE PETRIFIED FOREST

Yes, your Alchemist Magnet is here, and you'll also find a flask in a hole created by your hard landing. You should take the pine cone lying here. You'll need to get past the trees, but they won't budge to let you through. Come back to them later, after you've found a musical item that will make them feel like dancing,[1] and they'll let you pass.

THE BRIDGES OF KYRANDIA KOUNTY[2]

The knight, gentleman that he is, is a little one-sided. He won't let you pass to the left. Each time you try, he'll walk you back to the right side of the bridge. You've got to find some other pedestrian to distract the guard. Look around for a clue to the spell that can help you out. Hint: Think snow![3]

Once you've produced a stand-in pedestrian, give it to the knight, who will walk it across the bridge. Now you can go west, little Sheeba. Er, Zanthia.

THE FOOTPATH

Pretty chaotic scene, this one. As its name implies, there's a foot running circles on a path here, with two fellows trying to catch it. You need to talk to these two mystics, but you'll have to stop that foot somehow in order to get the mystics' attention. Check your spellbook for a clue on taking care of matters at hand (and foot) here. Hint: You need to do a good deed for the dull statue on the left.[4] Once you've cleaned up the situation, a Toy Box containing a magic drum and a single jack will appear. One of these items will put an end to all that running around behind you.[5]

After catching the foot, the mystics will explain that it once belonged to an ancient evil wizard named Bal-Rom, who was eventually blown to smithereens. After centuries of drifting in space, some of Bal-Rom's body parts have landed in Kyrandia. The most dangerous limb is—surprise!—Bal-Rom's left hand. The mystics warn that the hand will attempt to get its, well, hand, on the Wheels of Fate. Better bolt, babe. (Before you leave this scene, however, make sure you take the walnut growing beside the statue.)

THE TRAM

Sorry, no free rides here. The nutty squirrel intends to take his lunch break but won't leave while you're standing there. To get him to go away, you'll have to give him something. Actually, three things.[6] Once you send him away, you can use an item in your inventory to power the Tram wheel. Ready to roll?[7]

On the ride up, you'll encounter Marko and his heavy-handed Hand, battling in one of the Tram cars. The Hand will stop the tram and you'll have to climb the rest of the way to reach Alpinia, the next chapter in our tale.

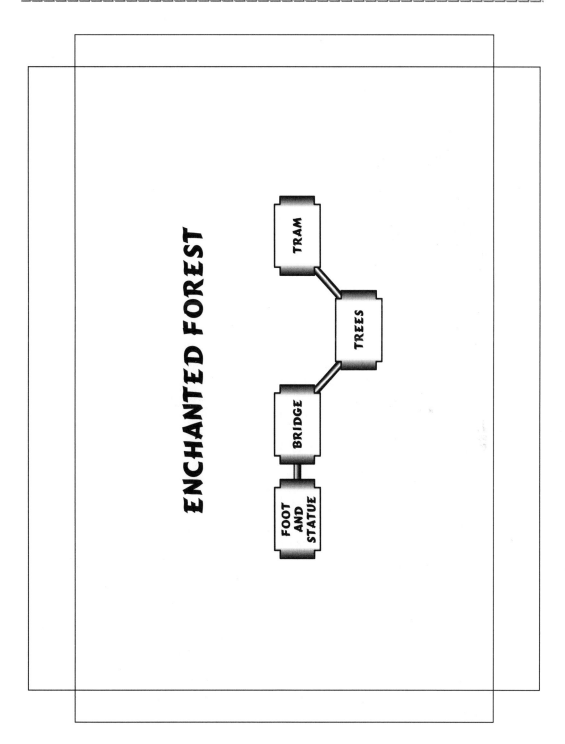

ENCHANTED FOREST

TRAM

TREES

BRIDGE

FOOT AND STATUE

CLUENOTES

1 The Toy Box, which you'll obtain at the statue near the Footpath by performing a good deed, contains the item you'll need to get to the root of the tree problem: A Drum.

2 No, the knight isn't really a photographer with whom you'll have a short but sweet affair, the likes of which will be turned into a best-selling little book, the success of which will astonish the critics, before it goes on to become a movie starring Meryl Streep and Clint Eastwood. That's not what's going on here at all. Thanks goodness for small miracles.

3 It's the Snowman spell. You'll need some snow, which you can get on the rise over the guard's head; some moss, which you can collect off the rock to the right of the bridge; and some charcoal. To make charcoal, you will need to burn the twigs. First, take the rest of the moss off that round rock to get a rolling rock. Take it. Next, go back to the trees. Place the twigs on the flintstone beside the trees, then apply the rolling rock to them. The rock will cause a spark that will ignite the twigs and burn them down to a lump of charcoal. *Voilà*. Now you have everything you need to make your pedestrian snowman.

4 The statue needs polishing. Your Alchemist's Magnet will work just fine.

5 Stick the jack in the path of the foot to cause it to stumble.

6 The pine cone that's lying near the trees, the acorn from near the bridge, and the walnut from beside the statue.

7 The rolling rock. Place it in the wheel and then hop aboard!

CHAPTER 11

ALPINIA

Okay, so you made it to the top of the Tram ride. Still, you're not high enough to reach the Hand of Fate. The first portion of this section is short and, well, sweet.

GETTING UPHILL

By the look of it, the hill to the south of the station is the way to the Wheels of Fate. All you need is some climbing gear. The snooty mother and her lip-smacking baby, eating a lollipop, won't offer any advice. The mother will just ignore you. Unless, that is, you can

charm her with a gift. Considering how often she checks herself in her mirror, something big and gaudy should work.[1]

THE SHOP

These two old farts won't have much more to offer than a few tasteless, chauvinistic clichés. When you ask to borrow their rope to climb the mountain, they refuse. A survey of the room reveals some cannonballs, a flask on the shelf, and some stuff in the wall-mounted yak's head. It's musk. Look in your spellbook and see which potion requires musk. That will be the potion you need to concoct to get rid of these two guys so you can take their rope.[2] Hint: Drink the potion outside, then come back into the shop.

THE REAL ABOMINABLE SNOWMAN

So much for climbing out of this place. Okay, that last stunt was really a trick, but this is the only way to move forward, honest. Outside the Snowman's cave, you can try to use some icicles as pitons to climb away; however Mr. Abominable won't let you get very far.[3] You need to distract him. Look around at what's inside his cave, and you'll figure out which potion to create. That is, *re*-create, since you just whipped up a batch of it moments ago.[4]

Once you've concocted the spell, use it outside at the right moment. Hint: Do you recall those hunters saying something about capturing Mr. Abominable?[5]

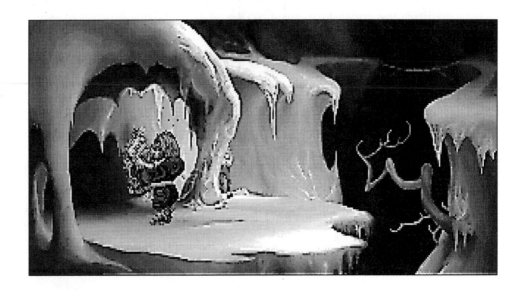

RAINBOW ROOM

Once you're up and away from Mr. A., you'll come to a small cabin. Inside, you'll find the famous Rainbow Room, where rainbows are created. By the looks of it, the troublesome Hand has sabotaged the Rainbow Machine. This is one heck of a puzzle. The bottom line: You need to restore all the colors of a rainbow on the tree. The colors, in their correct order, are: Red, Orange, Yellow, Green, Blue, Indigo, and Violet.

You'll need to create a potion in each of these colors, pouring each one as you complete it into one of the empty glass globes hanging on the tree. Luckily all the ingredients you'll need are here on the nine-slot shelf. Well, sort of. You'll have to work the levers to the left of the ingredients to switch the shelves and change which ingredients appear. By creating different combinations, you'll see different ingredients. As you change from one shelf collection to the next,

ingredients you've already used will be replenished. Use the flask in the shelf for collecting the potions you concoct. Hint: Empty it first by drinking the hot water.

Mixing Tip #1: After using a flask or bowl, place it in your inventory to use again, or toss it down the bottomless trash can to dispose of it.

Mixing Tip #2: For some ingredients, such as mustard, you'll need to combine two ingredients—ground radish and vinegar—to make the desired ingredient. Take the bowl of ground radish and put it in your inventory, then pour vinegar on it. You'll have mustard now, to put in your cauldron.

Mixing Tip #3: To change the lead heart to gold, put the lead heart in your inventory, then touch it with your alchemist magnet.

There's no simple clue to figuring out how to create the potions. Experimentation will pay off in the end. However, if you'd rather just get past this point, use the tables below to figure out how to change the shelves and which ingredients to use for the correct colored potions.

LEVER COMBINATIONS AND INGREDIENTS

LEVER	POSITION			
TOP	LEFT	fireberry	acorn	silver unicorn
MIDDLE	RIGHT	twigs	green crystals	hot water
BOTTOM	RIGHT	onion	domino	plant food
TOP	RIGHT	sulfur rock	lizard tears	rainbow stone
MIDDLE	RIGHT	black pebbles	toad stool	radish
BOTTOM	RIGHT	jack	ground grain	magnet
TOP	LEFT	bell	starfish	blueberries
MIDDLE	UP	hot air	broom	silver unicorn
BOTTOM	RIGHT	lollipop	anchor stone	amethyst
TOP	RIGHT	pine cone	mushroom	rolling stone
MIDDLE	UP	walnut	candle	gnarlybark
BOTTOM	RIGHT	ground radish	feathers	rainbow stone
TOP	LEFT	cheese	quill (feather)	domino
MIDDLE	RIGHT	moss	icicle	sweet & sour
BOTTOM	LEFT	orange peel	clam shell	gold coin
TOP	RIGHT	taffy	feathers	red cloth
MIDDLE	RIGHT	top hat	fuzz	stick
BOTTOM	LEFT	snowball	musk	root beer
TOP	LEFT	anchor	charcoal	footprint
MIDDLE	UP	sandwich	horseshoe	red leather
BOTTOM	LEFT	swamp water	lead	salt water
TOP	RIGHT	wool	drum	amethyst
MIDDLE	UP	ground grain	sand dollar	lead heart
BOTTOM	LEFT	lettuce	lollipop	vinegar

POTION RECIPES

The Red Potion is the Flying Shoes potion: Feather of Snipe, Red Leather Folio, and Hot Air.

The Orange Potion is the Sandwich Potion: Cheese, Lettuce, Ground Grain, and Mustard (Ground Radish and Vinegar combined in a bowl).

The Yellow Potion is the Abominable Snowman potion: Snow, Musk, Feathers, and Candy.

The Green Potion is the Swampsnake Potion: Onion, Sulfur Rock, Lizard Tears, Hot Water, Gnarlybark, and Toadstool (as in a little chair, not a mushroom).

The Blue Potion is the Teddy Bear Potion: Two Black Pebbles, Heart of Gold (the heart-shaped lead changed into gold with the Alchemist's Magnet), and Fuzz.

The Indigo Potion is the Indigo gem (purple) and Blueberries.

The Violet Potion is the Skeptic Serum: Sweet and Sour Sauce, Reptile Tears, Lucky Horseshoe, and Rabbit's Footprint.

CROSSING THE RAINBOW BRIDGE

Once you've filled the globes correctly, the machine will operate and produce a rainbow. You'll need to walk across the rainbow bridge to reach the Wheels of Fate. To get to the rainbow, use the icicle hanging in the right corner outside the building to climb onto the roof, then boogie on over the rainbow to the other side . . . .

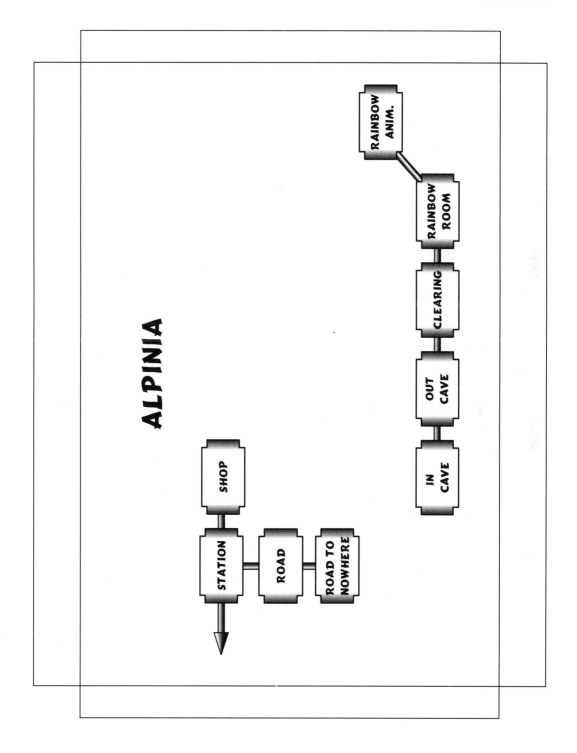

ALPINIA

CLUENOTES

1 Like a fat ball of gold, say? Inside the shop next door you'll find some lead cannon balls. Use your Alchemist's Magnet to turn one into gold and give it to Ms. Thing outside the Station. Who says money can't buy unhappiness?

2 Aha, the Abominable Snowman costume spell! You have the musk, taken from the yak's head. Snow is everywhere outside. Feathers are available from the feather duster hanging on the little Station shack. The last ingredient, Sugar, is a tough one. Then again, that baby was sucking a lollipop, wasn't he? See cluenote 1.

3 Use the icicle on the ice wall to the right of the cave. You'll be able to climb up and away eventually—after you distract Mr. Abominable, that is.

4 Create another Abominable Snowman potion. Use the cologne and candy from the cave, some feathers from the bed you were lying on, and some icicles from outside. There's a flask inside, behind Mr. A., but don't use the flask inside.

5 When the hunters show up outside the cave, use the potion on them.

CHAPTER 12

THE WHEELS OF FATE

Okay, Z. You've made it this far. After a little confrontation with Mr. Hand on the rainbow, you're ready for some real action. Get set for the final showdown.

THE DOORWAY

This one's easy. As you can see, the sun is bouncing off the gold reflector and onto the door, making it too hot to touch. Now, if that

reflector weren't made of gold, perhaps the door would cool down
enough to handle.[1]

THE CONTROL ROOM

In here, you'll finally discover what's been ailing Kyrandia: It's
missing its center wheel, as you can see by the empty spindle. You'll
have to find it and replace it to save Kyrandia. The missing wheel is
very close by, in . . .

THE MECHANIC'S ROOM (A.K.A. THE TOWERS OF ANNOY)

In the Mechanic's room, you would expect to find replacement parts;
however they're hidden. This giant puzzle works like the Tower of
Hanoi puzzle you may be familiar with, but upside down and
backwards. Only one disk may be moved at a time, and a smaller
disk cannot be placed on top of a larger disk. The object is to transfer
all of the disks from the right face to the left face to open the left lock,

then transfer all the objects from the left face to the middle face to open its lock. Each lock, when opened, will reveal an item to take.[2]

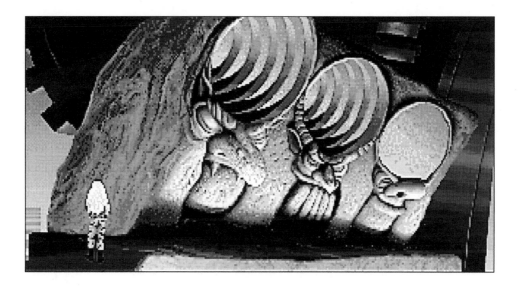

Important tip: Save your game before you try to solve this puzzle so you can start from scratch if you need to.

There are several ways to solve this puzzle, but if you're ready to get past it, here's the solution.

TOWERS OF ANNOY SOLUTION

From left to right, we have locks 1, 2, and 3. Perform the moves below in the following order solve the puzzle.

3 to 1	2 to 1	2 to 3	3 to 1
3 to 2	3 to 1	1 to 2	2 to 3
1 to 2	3 to 2	3 to 1	2 to 1
3 to 1	1 to 2	3 to 2	3 to 1
2 to 3	1 to 3	1 to 2	2 to 3

1 to 2	2 to 1	1 to 2	2 to 1
1 to 3	3 to 1	3 to 1	3 to 1
2 to 3	3 to 2	2 to 3	

After you complete the first part of the puzzle and open lock 1, save your game, then continue the puzzle, as follows, to move all of the disks in lock 1 to lock 2.

1 to 2	2 to 3	3 to 1	1 to 2
1 to 3	2 to 1	3 to 2	1 to 3
2 to 3	3 to 1	1 to 2	2 to 3
1 to 2	2 to 3	3 to 1	1 to 2
3 to 1	1 to 2	2 to 3	3 to 1
3 to 2	1 to 3	2 to 1	3 to 2
1 to 2	2 to 3	3 to 1	1 to 2
1 to 3	1 to 2	3 to 2	

FIXING THE MISSING WHEEL

Return to the control room with the stick and the missing wheel. Get ready for some action here—you're going to have to think and act fast once you get that wheel back in place. (This is a good time to save your game again.)

First, put the wheel on the empty spindle in the middle of the Kyrandia machine. Next, use the stick to leverage the wheel into place . . .

KYRANDIA IS SAVED!!!

But not for long. Moments after you fix the wheel, Mr. Hand will appear with a tied-up Marko. Now you must be quick on your feet. Your cue to move is the arrow cursor. When you see it "come back" on the screen after a move, move again, quickly.

The best strategy is to leap at the three-wheeled Kyrandia machine so that Mr. Hand misses you when he lunges. Then, when you square off with him again, click the cursor on him to belt him. He'll toss you around, but if you keep belting him, Marko will eventually get free and crawl on his hands and knees behind Mr. Hand. Hit Mr. Hand once more, and he'll trip over Marko, sending him flying over the edge of the deck. Wave bye-bye, Mr. Hand! This time, Z., Kyrandia really is saved! Give yourself a hand![3]

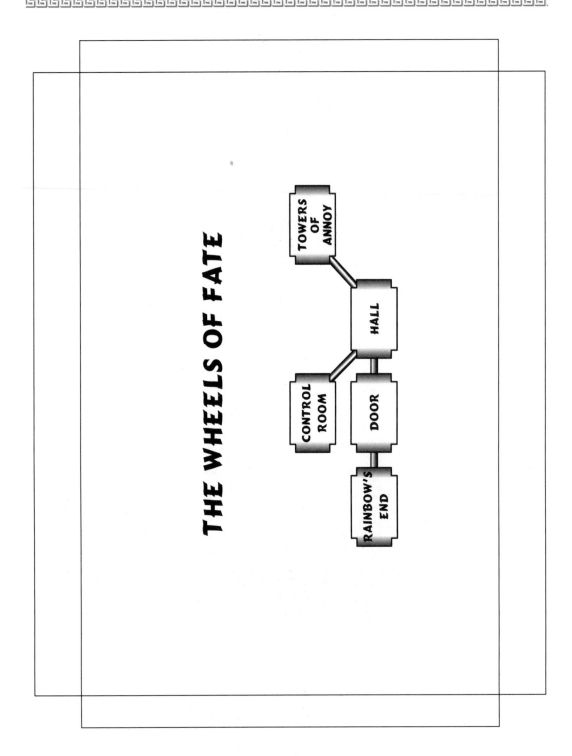

CLUENOTES

[1] Use your Alchemist's Magnet to turn the gold reflector into lead.

[2] Lock 1 will give up your friendly, loyal stick. Lock 2, the missing Kyrandia wheel.

[3] If you stick around through all of The Hand of Fate's final credits, you'll catch a haunting glimpse of what lies just around the corner . . . Kyrandia 3: Malcolm's Revenge.

BOOK 3

MALCOLM'S REVENGE

CHAPTER 13

HE-E-E-E'S BA-A-A-A-CK!

You, Malcolm, were a normal baby. Well, sort of. Your twofold conscience served to guide your actions. In your case, little man, resisting temptation was never easy. Your moral balance was tested frequently during your youth, and your dual consciences, Good vs. Evil (a.k.a. Stewart and Gunther, respectively) battled against one another constantly until your bad side eventually won out. As you grew into manhood, you became famous and successful in your own, notorious way. But with the news of your *supposed* slaying the King and Queen of Kyrandia, young Brandon, the heir to the thrown, put a stop to your madness. Finally, in the depths of your greatest humiliation, you were imprisoned in stone.

For a while, anyway . . . for as the people of Kyrandia sleep, a lucky bolt of lightning hits your stony shell, breaking you free. Surprise, surprise, look who's escaped! Now, finally, we can hear your side of the story!

MISSION OBJECTIVE

Your objective is to leave Kyrandia and get to the Isle of Cats. You're going to have to be very crafty and careful, for remember, your, shall we say, "tainted" reputation precedes you. If you are recognized by certain people who know you, you will be incarcerated and thrown into jail,[1] which will severely slow down your quest.

There are six ways to leave Kyrandia and reach the Isle of Cats. Wandering around and exploring first is a good way to find out what your options are. After you've stretched your legs some, you'll have a better idea of the challenges that lie ahead and the puzzles you'll need to solve.[2]

GENERAL TIPS

Here are some general tips to help you get started:

GOOD CONSCIENCE VS. BAD

Gunther, your bad conscience, will now and then make an appearance. Sometimes he pops in to toss off a comical comment on your actions, while at other times he's got some useful advice, if you listen carefully to what he says. Later in the game, your Good Conscience, Stewart, will make an appearance as well, and you'll have to choose between the two, or both consciences, to continue the game. Your choice will affect how the rest of the game plays out, but we'll get to that part in Chapter 17, when it's time to choose.

NAUGHTY VS. NICE (A.K.A. YOUR MOODMETER)

Your Moodmeter, in the lower right corner of the control screen, has three settings: Nice, Normal, and Lying. Depending on the situation you're in, you can get certain results by selecting certain settings. Sometimes being nice to people gets you help, but by the same token, lying may get you information or items. The reverse is also true: The wrong attitude can get you in trouble or prevent you from obtaining certain information or items. Experimenting with your Moodmeter when talking to people is one way to learn about its effects on others.[3]

PICKING LOCKS (OR NAILS)

Nails, which you can find at the dump whenever you go there, are useful for two things. (You can also pull a loose nail from the bleachers at the Town Arena.) First, the bent nail can be combined with your Nut-on-a-String (in your apartment) to create a Bent-Nail-on-a-String, which is useful for a number of tricks. With a bent or straight nail, you can unlock the Toy Factory, the Town Hall, and other locked doors you encounter. You can also use one to escape from prison in two situations that occur later in the game. When you use a straight nail on a lock, it winds up bent after the lock is unlocked and visa versa: a bent nail unbends after you use it on a lock. A bent nail is required for creating a Bent-Nail-on-a-String, but it makes no difference whether you carry a bent or straight nail for picking locks.

DISGUISES

Okay, so you've been warned to avoid people who might recognize you. That's still good advice, and by following it you may be able to leave Kyrandia sooner. Still, it's fun to play trick or treat, isn't it? By wearing costumes, you can fool people who would normally recognize you. Also, you'll be able to gather items from those you fool that you wouldn't be able to collect if you were to avoid them.

There are two kinds of disguises: partial and full. A partial disguise consists of one item, such as a wig, or something to cover part of your body. A full disguise means wearing both previously mentioned items, a wig and a body covering, or wearing the mime costume, which you can get by tricking the mime. (See "The Mime" for more details.)

The easiest partial disguise to procure involves a squirrel. You'll have to learn how to hypnotize one first, which is described in the section below, "Castle Dump." Full disguises involve tricking the mime or snatching a leather jerkin at the baths.

DEATH IS A LONELY BUSINESS

There are only a few ways to die in Malcolm's Revenge. In the unfortunate event of your death, a screen will appear, giving you the option to load a previously saved game or to choose "Second Chance" (except in Chapter 15 "The Ends of the Earth"), which will return you to the point just before your unexpected demise.

POINT POINTERS

Certain actions will gain you different kinds of points throughout the game. In general, the more dastardly or deviant the act, the more points you'll gain. While this is fun when it happens, don't concentrate on making points in the game—they're simply here for your entertainment and have no bearing on the completion of the game.

CASTLE DUMP

Search the dump carefully, and you'll find a number of items here.[4] Items that appear here vary. When you leave and come back, you will often find new or extra items.

As for that squirrel, you have quite a checkered history with these little creatures, making them vanish and whatnot. Don't mess with this one, though, if you know what's good for you.[5]

There is a way to tame the squirrel[6] so that you can use him for certain purposes.[7]

If you get thrown into prison and break free, come back to the Castle Dump to retrieve the items you had before you were tossed in jail.

THE BLUFF

Pretty view, isn't it? It can get really ugly if you find yourself alarming certain people you meet in Kyrandia. Simply put, here is where Herman, the local Lawman, will arrest you if someone in town recognizes you and sounds the town alarm. (We'll deal with Herman some more in the section titled "You're Under Arrest.")

THE PEGASUS LANDING

The first time you visit Pegasus Landing, you'll witness the arrival of Zanthia, our heroine from Kyrandia 2. Warning: Make sure your Moodmeter is set to Nice before visiting the Pegasus Landing the first time. She will not be pleased to see you. However if you are "Nice," she'll offer some helpful advice.[8]

THE GRAVE

This is where Queen Katherine, mother of Brandon, our heir-o of Kyrandia 1, is buried. If you touch her grave, a ghost will appear and suggest you place two flowers on the grave if you wish to speak to Katherine's spirit. A good idea, since Katherine, if you are "Nice" to her, will offer important information that you'll need later.[9]

Now, how to catch those darn flowers called Monkey Jumpers? Every time you try to pluck one, it scurries away, whimpering and crying. The trick is to cut them from their stems with a sharp object,

Pegasus Landing

rather than pluck them by hand. Have you found a sharp object or created one? The quickest way to find a sharp item is to revisit the Dump.[10]

Monkey jumper taken.

THE DOCK

Convincing the curiously-dressed Dog-Man at the Dock that you're part of the circus, or at least worthy of being part of it, is one way to get to the Isle of Cats. Talk to him and he will reveal that only circus people may board the boat. There is a disguise you can wear in order to "look" like you belong in the circus.[11] Or you can audition for the circus. Your specialty is juggling, so you'll have to make some juggling balls.[12]

Using your Bent-Nail-on-a-String, you can catch fish (actually, eels) here by standing on the low, right-side cliff and clicking on the sea.

THE MIME

Nobody loves a mime. You especially. However, this one is tougher than he looks. Push him too far and he'll let you have it.[13] No, you don't need this guy, but you could use what he's wearing, as a disguise to keep people who might recognize you from sounding the town alarm (see "You're Under Arrest"). Now, how to get him to shed his outfit? Staining it with a notoriously stinky item will work, but make sure his back his turned first, so you can slip the stinky item into his hood.[14]

Eel taken.

Once you get him in a stink, however, he won't just relinquish his suit to you. You'll have to retrieve it from the Bath House, which is where he runs off to.

THE BATH HOUSE

Getting inside here is easy, if you've got the right tool. Like most locks, this one will open with a bent nail, but not an ordinary bent nail.[15] Vince, the attendant here, will recognize you if you aren't wearing a disguise. (Actually, he's rather gullible, and by switching your Moodmeter to "Lying," you can fool him into believing you're not who he says you are.)

What you're interested in here is hanging in the Bath House window. If the mime ran in here, his clothes will be hanging in the window. If you come here before stinking up the mime's clothes, a leather jerkin[16] will be hanging in the window. In order to steal clothing hanging in the window, you'll need to distract Vince. To do this, try fiddling with the thermostat.[17] (Make sure your Moodmeter is set to Lying, so that you can convince Vince you're *not* fiddling with the meter, like he suspects.)

Mime outfit placed.

Once you cause a little temperature change, the crowd will go running from the bath house, causing the diversion you need to snatch the article hanging in the window. If it's two or three jerkins you're after (to use as leather with the Toy Making Machine in the Toy Factory), you can cause the same diversion again and again by leaving the Bath House and coming back again.

THE TOWN ARENA

There's not a lot of action here . . . not yet, anyway. Notice those two footprints? Later, when you meet Brandywine, you'll find out more about this place and what you can do here, if you've got the right potion. Hint: This makes a great teleportation pad.[18]

Portal potion taken.

DOWNTOWN KYRANDIA

You can reach Downtown Kyrandia, which is where you'll find your apartment and other places of interest, two ways: click on the center of the transport pod located on the Bluff to catapult yourself to Downtown Kyrandia; or travel south of the Bluff to the Outskirts of Town, then east to the Town Arena (click the giant frog statue to make it move out of your way), then east to the City Limits, then west into Downtown Kyrandia.

MALCOLM'S APARTMENT

You'll want to go to your apartment immediately to retrieve a few very useful items. Your apartment is located through the door in the rear of the Toy Factory. The Toy Factory is locked; however you can pick the lock with a nail. Ideally, you should use a straight nail so that after you pick the lock, the nail is bent.

Once you're in your apartment, use the bent nail with your Nut-on-a-String in your bureau drawer to create a Bent-Nail-on-a-String, which is useful for a number of tasks and tricks.[19]

Beneath the bed you'll find your Jester's Staff, which you can click on people to make them laugh. There are a few situations where making someone laugh will cause a distraction, giving you a chance to accomplish another task or trick.

Make sure you read the big purple album in the middle of your apartment. Pay particular attention to the last two pages of the book, as they'll give you some seedy tips that will come in handy later. (See "The Dairy" for more information.)

THE TOY FACTORY

There are a few points of interest here in the Toy Factory. First, there's the Toy Making Machine itself. By putting raw ingredients in its top golden funnel and pressing the green button on the right wall, the machine will produce a toy. The two knobs on the machine determine which toys it will make.

Toy Factory

To find out which lever combinations produce which toys, throw the levers up or down, then click on the big red book against the left wall. A blueprint of the toy will dance across the screen.

As for ingredients, wood[20] will create toy horses or soldiers, and leather[21] will create juggling balls. Placing these items in the machine, one item at a time, and arranging the levers correctly, as described above, then hitting the green button will produce the desired toy.

The toys you create have specific uses.[22]

The second point of interest in the Toy Factory is the hole in the floor, which will take you to the Cellar, beneath Town Hall.[23]

THE FISH CREAM PARLOUR

It's awfully crowded in here. The point of the Fish Cream Parlour is, of course, Fish Cream Sandwiches. That's what that big machine in the center of the bar is for. The only way to get the attention of Duane, the bartender, is by clearing the place out. You'll have to scare the customers away. To do this you'll need a rodent-like creature, but not a mouse. Subtle hint: Have you learned how to hypnotize a squirrel, yet? One of these little fellas, come undone, will do the trick.[24] Warning: Before you clear the place out, make sure you're wearing a disguise, or else Duane will sound the town alarm, causing your arrest the next time you enter the Bluff.

Once the place is empty you can talk to Duane. He'll tell you that he's all out of Fish Cream Sandwiches, but if you bring him the ingredients[25]—Fish (which in Kyrandia means Eel), Sesame, and Cream—he'll make you a sandwich. (There is an easier way to get a

Fish Cream Sandwich, however: Have you met the Foreign Exchange Student?)

Why do you want one of these disgusting sandwiches in the first place? Because they're useful for a number of situations.[26] Furthermore, you can substitute Squirrel for Eel and Duane will create a Squirrel Cream Sandwich. (As if Fish Cream Sandwiches aren't gross enough?) Brandywine, Darm's pet dragon, has a particular fondness for Squirrel in any form, and will trade valuable information for this, uh, delicacy.

THE FOREIGN EXCHANGE STUDENT

Now and then you'll run into a little kid wearing a red baseball hat, shorts, and red clogs. He may be from Holland; it's hard to say. One thing is for sure, he speaks a different language—one that you can't decipher, so don't bother trying.

Leather ball taken.

Offer him a toy,[27] and he'll give you a Fish Cream Sandwich in exchange. You'll have to persist with him in order to make the trade, and he may not do it the first few times you offer. If he doesn't, leave him, then find him and try again. Eventually, he'll do it.

THE DAIRY

Ah, smell that Dairy Air! There's a ton of sesame seed here, and equipment for feeding and milking cows. The sesame seeds are useful for creating Sesame Seed Bombs. [28] They're also one of the ingredients you'll need to give to Duane at the Fish Cream Sandwich Parlour to make Fish Cream Sandwiches. Cream is another ingredient, and to get some you'll need to lure the cows home.

Hint: If you add water to the sprouts, they germinate. Put enough germinated sprouts into the hopper and the cows'll come home.[29]

Once the cows are back, the milk machine will fill the large glass vat with cream. To get some cream, you'll need to puncture the vat carefully, then collect some cream in a glass flask.[30]

THE TOWN HALL

In here there's a big statue. The statue looks like he's eating and drinking. Notice the shape of the sandwich he's holding? Offering a similarly shaped food to the statue will have an interesting effect on it; however, this is not necessary yet.[31] (Later, near the very end of the game (in Chapter 17), this sort of offering is essential to your success.)

Fish cream sandwich taken.

The door on the rear wall is locked. Use a straight or bent nail to unlock it and gain access to the Cellar. (Some of the other doors around here stay unlocked once you open them, but this one must be unlocked every time you encounter it.)

THE CELLAR

It's damp and dark and wet down here, but this is a place you'll visit often. Notice the puddle to the right? A little fishing here will yield you as many eels as you want. Do you have a fishing pole? No? Well, a string with a hook will do.[32]

Empty flask dropped.

If you look closely, you'll see that a few things seem out of place here. The first is that crumbly brick wall, on the left. Tearing it down will gain you access to the Catacombs and something precious inside.[33] To tear down the wall, you'll need to combine sesame seeds with eel to produce fertilized sesame seed, which turns into Sesame Seed Bombs under the right circumstances. With the fertilized seed and another item that's plentiful here, you can tear down the wall, providing you place the seeds correctly then activate them correctly.[34]

DARM'S HOUSE

By touching first the green apple, then the red one, on the rug in the Cellar, you will be transported to Darm's House. Warning: Don't enter Darm's House unless you're wearing a partial disguise or else he'll kick you out at once and sound the town alarm.

Old Darm will think you are the sandwich delivery boy. Have you a sandwich to offer? Once you offer him one, he'll talk to you. He'll tell you that Brandywine has been bad.

Talk to Brandywine the dragon, too. (Make sure your Moodmeter is set to Normal.) She'll tell you that she's been grounded because Darm's accused her of using Portal Potions to visit the Isle of Cats. Aha! Portal Potions! You can get more information out of Brandywine if you can somehow force Darm to leave the room. Hint: Darm loves a good laugh—actually, more than one good laugh.[35]

Better still, Brandywine will tell you an incredibly valuable secret—a super speedy way to reach the Isle of Cats—if you give her something that will make her very happy. Hint: Brandywine has an appetite for furry-tailed creatures.[36]

THE CATACOMBS

There's only one thing in here that you care about: Brandywine's Portal Potion. It's in the lovely green flask. Use an empty flask to collect some, then take it to the Town Arena and drink the Portal Potion.[37] Away!

Portal potion taken.

THE MAGICIAN'S LODGE (ZANTHIA'S PLACE)

Unless you're wearing full disguise costume when you come in here, Zanthia will recognize you and sound the town alarm—the next time you visit the Bluff, Herman will arrest you. (The only reason to come here in the first place is if you want to use Zanthia's magic Pegasus Potion to leave Kyrandia rather than one of the other methods. If you've already determined another way to leave, such as Brandywine's Portal Potion, or by auditioning for the circus, you can skip the Magic Lodge altogether.)

The Lodge won't be open until you encounter Zanthia for the first time at the Pegasus Landing. If your meter is on Nice when you meet her there, she'll give you some good advice on how to leave Kyrandia (make sure you're not wearing that silly Squirrel cap, though, or else she won't tell you).

Rocking horse taken.

After encountering Zanthia at the Pegasus Landing, you can find her in the Magic Lodge, busily concocting some sort of potion. When you talk to her (providing you are wearing a full disguise), she'll mention an ingredient the potion needs—Essence of Horse. Can you find a substitute?[38] Once you have an item that will work, you'll need to distract Zanthia from her cauldron so you can add the item to the potion then snatch some in a flask. Have any of those sesame bombs handy?[39]

Once you've got the Pegasus Potion, take it to the Pegasus Landing and drink it to leave Kyrandia and reach the Isle of Cats.

Pegasus potion taken.

YOU'RE UNDER ARREST

If someone recognizes you as the dastardly Malcolm, they'll signal the town alarm, alerting Herman of your presence. The alarm isn't something you'll hear. But you'll know it's been sounded when someone who recognizes you tosses you from their premises. These folks include Duane the Fish Cream Parlour bartender, Vince the Bath House attendant, Darm the Wizard, and Zanthia the Alchemist. The first three, Duane, Vince, and Darm, can be fooled by a partial disguise.[40] Zanthia (whom you'll first encounter at the Pegasus

Landing and later in her Magic Lodge), however, will recognize you in a simple disguise. To fool her, you'll need to wear a full disguise.[41]

Bluff

Once the town alarm has been sounded, you will be arrested by Herman, the lawman, the next time you arrive at the Bluff, where he's waiting for you.

DEALING WITH HERMAN

When you arrive at the Bluff, Herman will come racing after you to arrest you, then take you to Kallak and Brandon for your sentencing. You can evade Herman the first time he tries to catch you by preparing a trick that he'll run into and stumble over. Remember those firewood logs? Placing one in Herman's path *before* you are arrested will trip up the lawman, allowing you to make your escape.

Next time you return, however, Herman will be ready for you with a net. You can foil him a second time if you are carrying a sharp object in your hand *before* you return to the Bluff. With the sharp

item *in hand*, you'll cut your way out of the net after Herman tosses it over your head.

Sharp objects that will work include a toy soldier, a broken flask, scissors (which you can get the first time you're are imprisoned), or shears (which you can get the third time you're imprisoned, assuming you've escaped the first two prison situations).

Bluff

The third time you return, however, Herman will use a Magic Restraint Hold on you, from which you cannot escape. Oh well, a good thing never lasts, right? If you keep getting recognized, you're going to have to serve time anyway. Once you do, though, knowing how to escape each incarceration will move things along more quickly and eventually land you on the Isle of Cats—if, that is, you decide to take this criminal route to get there instead of one of the other puzzle options.

HIDING AN ESCAPE ITEM (IMPORTANT!!!)

When Herman catches you, he'll take you to Kallak and Brandon, who will describe your sentence and give you a little grief. After they've said their peace, Herman will tell you to put your items into

Brandon and Kallak

the box sitting on the ground. He'll warn you not to try hiding an item in your hand.

Important: Don't listen to him! You do *want to hide something in your hand before he carts you off to your prison situation. Depending on which prison situation you're being sent to (see below), make sure you pick up the appropriate "escape item" from your inventory. You'll have five seconds to do this, so make sure you click it as soon as he tells you to put your things in the box, then just wait. After five seconds, he'll send you to your prison situation, at which you'll arrive with the item you "held" in your inventory, ready to use to escape.*

PRISON SITUATIONS

Each time you are arrested you'll be sent to one of four prison situations. They are the Doily Factory, the Quarry, the Chain Gang, and the Galley.

Bent nail taken.

At each prison situation you'll be assigned menial, repetitive task to perform. Once you complete your task, you'll be returned to Kyrandia, and Herman will give you back your items.

By escaping a prison situation, you can skip the menial task and return to Kyrandia at once, advancing the "prison situations" system, so that the next time you're arrested, you wind up at the next prison situation in a series of four (or the Isle of Cats, if you escape the last situation, "The Galley").

In order to escape a prison situation, you'll need to be holding a special "escape item," as described in the first line of each prison escape, below.

Once you're back in Kyrandia, as long as you avoid being recognized by someone, you won't be sent to another prison situation. However, if you are recognized, you'll be sent back to the Doily Factory, or, if you escaped the Doily Factory, to the next prison situation in the series. By escaping each prison situation, as described below in "Prison Escapes," you'll be moved to the next situation, until you reach the last one, "The Galley." By escaping the last prison situation, you'll be transported to the Isle of Cats.

PRISON ESCAPES

By following these instructions, you can escape each prison situation. The first line for each escape lists the item you'll need to have on you when Herman sends you off to the described prison situation. If you don't have the item in hand, you won't be able to escape—make sure you click on it so that it's "in your hand" when Herman tells you to put your items into the box.

After escaping the Doily Factory or the Chain Gang, you can recover your confiscated items at the Castle Dump.

Portal potion taken.

THE DOILY FACTORY

Escape item: Straight or bent nail (but not a Bent-Nail-on-a-String).

Ten doilies. That's how many you have to make. Rowena will tell you how to make your first. After that, she'll split, leaving you to your own devices. Did you sneak a nail in with you when Herman told you to put your things in the box? That's the trick to your escape here. If you have a nail with you, you can escape, without having to make nine more doilies.

Here's the breakout plan: Use the nail to pick the lock on the doily-making machine. Zow! Check out this dude! (This rest isn't going to be pleasant, but I assure you he won't be permanently injured.) Now, take the scissors and stick the freak in the doily machine with them. Put the string in the machine, then step on the pedal to get the machine going. The freak will string together a long rope of doily string that'll fall out the window. Now, climb out—but snatch the scissors before you climb out if you want, since they're handy for foiling Herman's net if he tries to capture you with it.

Once you're back in Kyrandia, you can recover your confiscated items from the Castle Dump.

THE QUARRY

Escape item: Fertilized seeds (that is, sesame seeds combined with an eel that you caught at the Docks or in the Cellar using your Bent-Nail-on-a-String).

Look who's here: Rowena! You got her in hot water by busting out of the Doily Factory. Oh well, seems like she's only got eyes for you anyway. Lucky stiff! Back to work: You'll have to break ten boulders here and cart them to the funnel. Pain in the neck. Unless you escape, of course.

Fertilized seeds taken.

Breakout plan: Take the fertilized seeds you smuggled in and place them between the boulders. Next, click on yourself to wipe sweat on the seeds and make them sprout. *Voilá*! The seeds will knock all the boulders into the funnel, and you'll be free! When you return to Kyrandia, Herman will give you back your stuff and tell you to get out of Kyrandia.

THE CHAIN GANG

Escape item: None. You'll find pruning shears for your escape in this prison situation.

Pruning shears taken.

Well, well, look how close you and Rowena are becoming! The task here is to prune the bush ten times. Unless, of course, you escape.

Breakout plan: Use the pruning shears to cut your chains loose. Important: Cut the chain connecting Rowena and the guy next to you, freeing Rowena first, so that she can cause a diversion, allowing you to escape unnoticed.

If you like, you can take the Pruning Shears with you and use them to escape from the fourth prison situation, the Galley. A bent or straight nail will work for the Galley escape as well.

Once you're back in Kyrandia, you can recover your confiscated items from the Castle Dump.

THE GALLEY

Escape item: A nail (bent or straight) or pruning shears taken from The Chain Gang.

Pruning shears taken.

This is it, your last prison situation. Isn't that Rowena a beaut? You're ordered to row the great oar. After the first stroke, the guard will tell you that you have 999 more to row! Yow! Fortunately, this isn't the case: You only have to row 13 more strokes to be paroled back to Kyrandia. But why would you want to do that when you can escape—and this time for good, to the Isle of Cats!

Breakout plan: Use a nail to pick the lock or pruning shears to cut the chain.

Finally, the Isle of Cats! Proceed to the next chapter!

LEAVING KYRANDIA

There are six ways to leave Kyrandia and reach the Isle of Cats. They are:

#1 Getting arrested, and thrown into, then escaping, each prison situation. See "You're Under Arrest" to learn about the prison situations and how to escape each.

#2 Auditioning for the circus for the Dog at the Docks. You'll need three juggling balls, which you can make in the Toy Factory using three leather items. Make sure you're Moodmeter is set to Lying or else the Dog won't believe you.

#3 Trick the Dog at the Docks into thinking you are a Mime by wearing the Mime's costume. See "The Mime" for details on how to get the Mime's clothes. (While the Dog will fall for this disguise, he won't let you board the Circus boat until you bring him a Fish Cream Sandwich.)

#4 Drink a Pegasus Potion at the Pegasus Landing. See "The Magician's Lodge" for more information on how to create the Pegasus Potion.

#5 Drink a Portal Potion at the Town Arena to teleport yourself to the Isle of Cats. See "Darm's House" for more information on how to get the Portal Potion.

#6 Give Brandywine a hypnotized squirrel or a Squirrel Cream Sandwich and she'll tell you a secret and speedy way to leave: By clicking two eels together and saying "I want to go to the Isle of Cats." Make sure your Moodmeter is set to Normal. See "Darm's House" for more information.[42]

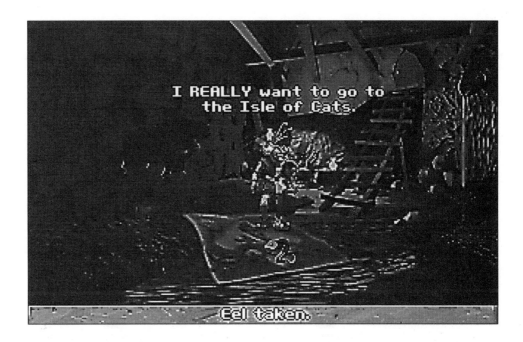

Any one of the above options will enable you to say good-bye to Kyrandia...for a while, anyway—you'll be back for the finale, in Chapter 17, "Back To Kyrandia."

Don't worry about having any items with you before you leave Kyrandia for the Isle of Cats. None of the items you've gathered on Kyrandia are necessary on the Isle of Cats.

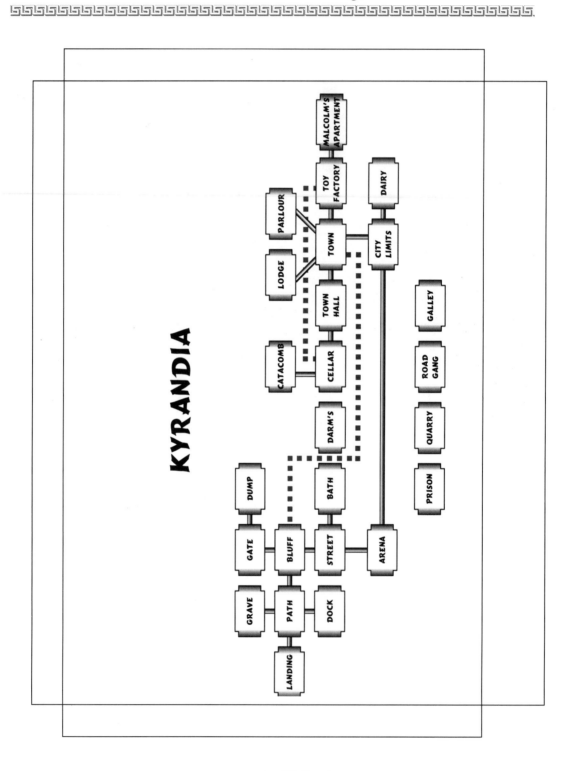

KYRANDIA

CLUENOTES

1 If you entirely avoid Zanthia, Darm, Vince the Bath House attendant, and Duane at the Fish Cream Parlour, then the authorities (in this case, Herman) won't be alerted that you've returned. You may wish to be in contact with these people, however, depending on which course you take to leave Kyrandia and reach the Isle of Cats. The only way to make safe contact with Zanthia, Duane, and Darm is by wearing a disguise. You may wear a disguise for Vince; however simply lying to him will work as well.

2 If, after wandering around, you become frustrated or simply want to know your six options for leaving Kyrandia, skip to the end of this chapter to the section titled "Leaving Kyrandia."

3 Being Nice to Katherine's ghost will yield some tips on how to escape Kyrandia; speak to Brandywine with a Normal setting and you'll get good advice; be Nice to Zanthia when you first encounter her at the Pegasus Landing and she'll go a little easier on you; you'll need to Lie to Vince the Bath House attendant to fool him about your true identity, and Lie to the Dog-Man at the Dock if you decide to audition for the circus or impersonate the mime.

4 A leather shoe, some nails for picking locks, some orange peels, a broken saw, a flask or two for holding water and potions, and some broken flasks (which you can use to cut and capture those run-away flowers). Make sure you have two nails on you when you start the game. The orange peel is useless except for using as a "gag" on yourself.

5 Basically, he'll bite your head off. Hey, you were warned, big guy.

6 You can lure him closer by placing some sesame seeds, found in the dairy, to the left of the log he's standing on, then hypnotize him with your Nut-on-a-String, which you'll find in your apartment.

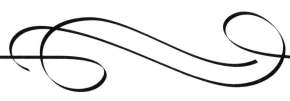

7 Squirrels are handy for making Squirrel Cream Sandwiches; for feeding to Brandywine at Darm's hut, in exchange for some very useful information; or for wearing on your head as a disguise. To remove a squirrel you're wearing as a hat, click the Nut-on-a-String or Bent-Nail-on-a-String on him and he'll scurry off your head and away to safety. Each time you hypnotize a squirrel and take it, another squirrel will appear at the Dump when you leave and come back to it.

8 She'll flat-out suggest that you leave by way of the circus boat at the Docks, by auditioning for the circus with a juggling act, or that you get an outfit and bluff your way on board.

9 "Only a Royal Séance can bring his ghost back now," Katherine says, referring to King William, whom you'll need to contact in this fashion at the end of the game, in Chapter 17.

10 Where you'll most likely find a broken flask. If there isn't one there, leave and come back once or twice; eventually one will be there. Use this to cut free two flowers. Another sharp object that will work is a toy soldier (see "The Toy Factory").

11 The Mime costume. If you wear it, he'll let you board — but only after you bring him a souvenir: a genuine, Kyrandian Fish Cream Sandwich.

12 Have you visited the Toy Factory yet? With three leather items you can make three juggling balls, with which you can audition for the circus. When you audition, make sure you Moodmeter is set to Lying.

13 As in, he'll shoot you dead with a make believe arrow that's all too real.

14 An eel, which you can catch in the Cellar, or at the Dock using you Bent-Nail-on-a-String.

15 Use your Bent-Nail-on-a-String to jimmy the Bath House lock open.

16 Which you can use at the Toy Factory to create a leather juggling ball, or wear as a partial disguise. Wearing a jerkin and a squirrel cap together make up as a full disguise.

17 Click it twice on either blue, for cold, or red, for hot, to make the temperature inside unbearable.

18 Brandywine will tell you about the Portal Potion, which, if you consume it here, will teleport you to the Isle of Cats. The Portal Potion is hidden in the room on the other side of the crumbly brick wall in the Cellar.

19 The plain old Nut-on-a-String or Bent-Nail-on-a-String can be used to hypnotize squirrels at the dump. The Bent-Nail-on-a-String can also be used to catch fish at the Dock or in the puddle in the Cellar below Town Hall, and to pick the lock at the Bath House gate.

20 There's firewood at the Outskirts of Town, in front of the Dairy.

21 The old shoe you found in the Dump at the start of the game is leather. The jerkin, hanging in the Bath House window, is leather, (and also acts as a partial disguise if you wear it, or as a full disguise if you wear it while wearing a hypnotized squirrel on your head). You can get two more of these by pulling the stunt described in "The Bath House" twice. And hypnotized squirrels, I am sorry to say, are considered leather in this twisted world. Blech! (At least they're not aware of what's happening to them when you toss them in . . .)

22 Three juggling balls will let you audition for the circus at the Dock. Make sure you Moodmeter is set to Lie before you juggle. Any of the toys can be offered to the wandering Foreign Exchange Student in exchange for Fish Cream Sandwiches. He won't make the trade at first, but if you are persistent, he'll eventually give in. toy soldiers can be used as sharp objects for cutting down a few of those hard-to-catch flowers, or for freeing yourself from Herman's net if he captures you with it at the Bluff.

23 You can also get to the Cellar by entering the Town Hall. Both the Cellar door in Town Hall, and Town Hall itself, are locked, and you'll need a bent or straight nail to pick the locks and get inside.

24 Put a hypnotized Squirrel on the floor here then de-hypnotize it with the Nut-on-a-String or Bent-Nail-on-a-String. It will run around wildly, scaring off the customers.

25 The eel you can catch in the puddle in the Cellar or in the sea at the Docks, using your Bent-Nail-on-a-String. Sesame seeds are plentiful in the Dairy, and cream you''ll have to get by luring the cows back into the Dairy, and then gathering some cream in a flask. (See "The Dairy.")

26 The Sculpture in Town Hall will awaken if you give him a Fish Cream Sandwich; Darm will crave one before he speaks with you (disguised); and the Dog at the Dock will require one if you're trying to join the circus masquerading as the mime, in its costume that you stole.

27 He seems to prefer a leather ball to a rocking horse or a toy soldier, but you may have to try all three until he accepts one of them.

28 Sesame Seed Bombs let you overturn objects, such as the tall cabinet in Zanthia's lab, which will distract her from her potion, or let you break down the wall in the Cellar, to reach the Catacomb. To create a Seed Bomb, combine some sesame seed with a fish, which you can catch in the little puddle in the Cellar using your Bent-Nail-on-a-String. The fish/sesame seed will yield fertilized seeds which, when you add water to them, sprout wildly, knocking items over or out of its way.

29 You'll need to toss a total of five small sprouted sesame seed batches into the hopper to bring home the cows, or two large sprouts, which you can make with fertilized seeds. (Fertilized seeds are created by mixing sesame seed with eel, which you can catch in the Cellar by clicking your Bent-Nail-on-a-String on the puddle of water, or by clicking the same make-shift fishing gear on the water at the Docks.)

30 Use a nail to puncture the vat and start a stream of cream flowing. Be careful not to make a second puncture — if you do, the machine will explode all over you!

31 Give the dude a Fish Cream Sandwich and he'll wake up, thank you very much, then go back to his solid state. A waste of a Fish Cream Sandwich — unless you're at the end of the game, when you'll need to offer him one.

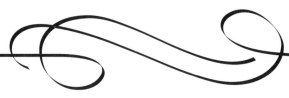

32 Actually, your Bent-Nail-on-a-String works just fine for catching eels at either the Dock or in the Cellar.

33 The Portal Potion, which, when used while standing on the footprints at the Town Arena, will teleport you directly to the Isle of Cats.

34 Place fertilized seeds in the middle of the loose brick wall, then pour a flask of water, taken from the puddle, on the seeds.

35 Three, in fact. Tickle the old man three times with your Jester's Staff, and he'll laugh so hard he'll have to leave the room, giving you an opportunity to talk to Brandywine in private. She'll tell you about Portal Potions.

36 As in squirrels. You can give her a hypnotized one or a Squirrel Cream Sandwich, made the same way as a Fish Cream Sandwich (but substitute hypnotized squirrel for eel). Give one to her, and she'll tell you a speedy way to leave Kyrandia and reach the Isle of Cats without jumping through a ka-jillion hoops, like you've done so far. (The secret isn't listed here is because it only works if you actually give Brandywine the squirrel.)

37 Don't worry about standing exactly on the two footprints in the Town Arena. As soon as you drink the potion, you'll automatically walk to the footprints and then get carried away.

38 Make a toy rocking horse at the toy shop.

39 Fertilize some sesame seeds with a fish caught in the Cellar or at the Docks. Place the fertilized seeds beneath the magic cabinet in Zanthia's Magic Lodge, then pour a flask of water on the seeds to overturn the cabinet. This will distract Zanthia so you can drop in the rocking horse and get some Portal potion for yourself.

40 For example, wearing a hypnotized squirrel on your head or a leather jerkin on your body.

41 Meaning, you'll have to get the Mime's costume and wear it yourself. See "The Mime" for more details. Or you can wear a leather jerkin and a hypnotized squirrel, which, together, comprise a full disguise.

42 Simply clicking two eels together without first "hearing" this secret from Brandywine herself won't do; you'll have to hear it straight from the horse's, er, dragon's, mouth in order to make the secret work.

CHAPTER 14

THE ISLE OF CATS

Ah! You're finally in the tropics! But what a strange place this is. You'll meet a cast of oddball characters here, all caught up in a war between the beasts. There are a few serious dangers here, and although the Isle isn't that big, finding your way around can get a little confusing. Follow the map closely when traveling the jungle and you shouldn't get lost very often. Let's start hiking.

MISSION OBJECTIVE

Your objective is to plot your revenge against Kyrandia. You're main goal here is to recruit a few thugs to assist you in an attack on

Kyrandia. In order to recruit the thugs, (a.k.a. the Pirates), you'll have to show their leader a little magic. And to acquire a magical item, you'll have to solve the colossal Cat Colossus puzzle.

GENERAL TIPS

Here are some tips to help you get started on The Isle of Cats.

ARRIVING ON THE ISLAND

How you left Kyrandia will determine where you land on the Isle of Cats. The ideal place to land is the Dog Fort, where there's a machete lying on the ground that you can take. You'll need to acquire this handy item before you can do much else here. If you arrive in the dark room, leave the room to the left and you'll be at Dog Fort.

If you didn't arrive at Dog Fort, you'll need to hitch a ride there, as described below in "Cat Cart Rides," before you go anywhere else.

Machete taken.

CAT CART RIDES

If you arrived at the Altar of Cats, or at the Pirate Beach, talk to the dog sitting on the cat-drawn cart. If you are "Nice," he'll give you a ride when you click the cart itself. Where he'll take you is random—each ride can land you in one of two places. You may have to take more than one ride, one after the other, to get to the desired location.

During the ride you can skip the cinematic jungle travel sequences by hitting the Esc *key.*

Cat Cart rides will only take you to and from other Cat Cart locales. These include Pirate Beach, the Altar of Cats, and Dog Fort. Other locations, such as the Colossus Statue, Fluffy's Hideout, and the Cave (with its second, Hieroglyphics room) can all be reach by foot from

Cat Cart locations (see map). Unfortunately, the jungle can only be traveled by foot.

Feel free to engage both the cat and the dog in conversation to hear both sides of the Cats vs. Canines War.

ISLAND DANGERS

There are three things to watch out for here. First, there are the Kissing Snakes, which, as their name implies, will kiss you to death. You'll need to kill these with a machete, which you can find at Dog Fort. Without the machete, you won't get very far in the jungle before encountering your first Kissing Snake death.

Second, the Island is infested with fleas. Every time you visit Dog Fort you'll attract fleas, even though you won't see them jump on

Mysterious Jungle

your body. When you see yourself start scratching, that's the first sign of infestation.

You must rid yourself of fleas periodically, or else you'll scratch yourself to death. To remove the fleas, click on yourself to pick off fleas (and drop them on the ground) or jump into one of the puddles you'll encounter in the jungle for a quickie flea dip.

If you see yourself beginning to scratch wildly, make sure you get rid of your fleas fast or else you'll die very soon.

Third, if you arrive on the Isle of Cats in the dark cave, or enter it from Dog Fort, don't go down the steps to your right or else you'll stumble to your death. The only way to go down to the Cat Hieroglyphics Room safely is by clearing some overhead brush that will let light in and brighten the way.[1]

JUNGLE TRAVEL

Traveling the jungle is complicated. Use the map to track your place. Even with this handy guide, you may eventually wind up lost. You'll need to explore the jungle to find dog bones, which you'll use at the Dog Fort to uncover gems (see "The Dog Fort"). To clear a path in the jungle, you'll need the machete, which you can find at Dog Fort. The machete is also useful for hacking away any kissing snake whose nest you uncover. Do them in quickly or else they'll jump onto you and kiss you to death.

THE DOG FORT

If this isn't where you arrive to when you come to the Isle of Cats, you should definitely make it your first destination—and get here as soon as possible. See that machete lying near the rear fence? Take it. You'll need it to kill snakes in the jungle and to chop down jungle bushes that block your path.[2]

Bone taken.

DOG BONES AND GEMS

As you clear jungle brush you'll occasionally find a dog bone. Collect these and bring them back to Dog Fort. The first time you give the dog a bone, he'll dig up a red gem for you. The next time you give him a bone he may or may not dig up a gem for you. A total of six gems are buried here, in fifteen possible locations. The trick here is this: If you simply give the dog a bone, he'll dig wherever he wants. You must direct him to where you want him to dig by placing the bone on that location.

The best strategy is to start from the top part of the digging area, placing bones left to right and down as you go. Eventually, after a number of misses, the dog will dig up all six gems that are hidden here.[3]

By following the "dog bone search circuit," you can quickly find lots of bones without having to delve too deeply into the complicated jungle. To perform the circuit, follow the map closely in this order: Dog Fort to Jungle 2 (right), then (up) to Jungle 4, then (left) back to Jungle 2, then (right) back to Dog Fort.

Once you have all six gems you can use them at the Colossus Ruins.

RETRIEVING LOST GEMS

If you inadvertently give the Pirates some or all of your gems, you can recover them from the ship's cargo hold. To get onto the ship, however, you'll have to boot the Captain off, at least temporarily. Notice how he keeps scratching himself? Perhaps if you can make him scratch even more, so much so that he goes crazy, he'll abandon ship long enough for you to get your gems from the barrel in the cargo hold below.[4]

Amethyst taken.

PIRATE BEACH

Aye, thar's four Pirates here, and one is clearly in charge. Won't this bunch and their sea-worthy ship make the perfect team for your attack on Kyrandia? Indeed.

Captain Jean Claude says he's at your service; however, he'll point out that Kyrandia is not a good place to attack without magic. Begging won't help matters. The Captain says show him some magic first, and then you and his crew can go.

Machete taken.

If you try to board the ship while the Captain is on it, he'll tell you you're not allowed on here. You can get past him, but you'll have to distract him in some way. Have you noticed how he keeps itching his back? If you were to make him even more itchy, he'd have to abandon ship and take a dip.[5]

FLUFFY AND THE CAT CAUSE

Fluffy is always to the right of the Altar of Cats. (You can get back to the Altar of Cats by hacking away the bushes to the right side of the screen, and taking that path.)

Fluffy will tell you about his Revolution. If you are sympathetic to his cause he'll give you a useful item—but only if you are sympathetic![6]

THE ALTAR OF CATS

Depending on how you left Kyrandia, you may wind up here first. If you haven't been to the Dog Fort yet, hitch a ride there by being nice to the Cat Cart driver. (See "General Tips," above, for more info on how to get started on the Isle of Cats.)

True to your first intuition, something is supposed to be placed on the altar. Actually, six items.[7] They don't belong there, but by placing each of the six things on the Altar, one at a time, you'll receive six important clues that will help you solve the Colossus Ruins puzzle.

With the six clues you get here, combined with the clues you get in the Cat Hieroglyphics Room, you're ready to solve the Colossus Ruins puzzle.

THE CAT HIEROGLYPHICS ROOM

To get to the Cat Hieroglyphics Room, enter the cave beside the guard dog at Dog Fort. The Ruins will be dark inside, and you won't be able to descend the stairs (to the right) unless you brighten the room first.

Hint: In a nearby forest location bushes are blocking a hole in the ground that normally admits sunlight into this room.[8] You'll have to

clear the jungle bushes from the hole before you can safely enter the Cat Hieroglyphics Room.

Once you've lightened the Ruins Room, you'll be able to proceed down the steps and to the right, into the Hieroglyphics Room. It's very dark in here when you first enter. A special item, when clicked on the dark hieroglyphic wall, will brighten up the place.

Hint: Cats absolutely love chasing after and eating the likeness of this particular item.[9]

Clicking the item again on each of the six hieroglyphics will offer six clues which, when combined with the clues you learn at the Altar of Cats, will help you solve the Colossus Ruins puzzle.[10]

Make a note of each hieroglyphic's associated gem, and then visit the Altar of Cats if you have not already, for six more clues that will enable you to solve the Colossus Ruins puzzle.

THE COLOSSUS RUINS

The Colossus Ruins lie to the left of the Altar of Cats. The statue, which is in the shape of a mouse, is two screens wide. Traveling to the right will take you to the right side. Notice it is surrounded by six spheres. Well, let's see. Six spheres. Six gems. Sounds like a match. Sort of. First, you'll have to figure out a way to "activate" the spheres.[11] Hint: Have you visited Fluffy yet and told him that you are sympathetic to his cause?

Second, you'll have to figure out which gem belongs to which cat statue. Hint: Visit the Altar of Cats with your six gems. Also: Visit the Hieroglyphics Room with the item that Fluffy gave you.

Once you've restored the six surrounding spheres to each their original statuesque forms, you must place, in the correct order, one gem in each statue's breastplate.

Warning: You must give the correct gems in the correct statues.[12] If, upon placing the sixth gem, you have not put them in their correct

Colossus Ruins

order, an explosion will occur, causing the gems to fly into various parts of the jungle. You'll have to search the jungle to recover them and try again.

Cat Colossus

With all six gems in their correct place, the mouse statue will glow and produce a magical Crystal Mouse, with which you can now prove your magical abilities to the pirates.[13] As you make your way to Pirate Beach, you may notice that things have changed on the Isle of Cats.[14]

LEAVING THE ISLE OF CATS

Once you've solved the Colossus Ruins puzzle, you'll have the item you need for proving your magical abilities to the Pirates which will allow you to leave the Isle of Cats. Only one of the pirates will hold still and let you try out your new magic device on him.[15] Once you've proven yourself, you and your motley crew will set sail for Kyrandia!

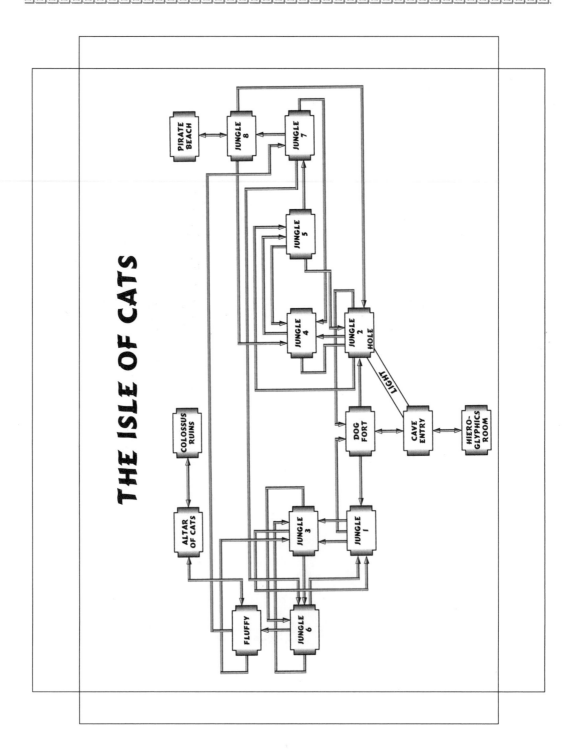

THE ISLE OF CATS

CLUENOTES

1 Clear the brush in Jungle 2 (on the map) with your machete so that light can enter the hole in the ground. Once that's clear, you can enter the cave at Dog Fort and then go down into the Cat Hieroglyphics Room (right) safely without breaking your neck.

2 Clearing jungle bushes is also how you'll find dog bones, which you'll give to the dog here to have him dig up the six gems you'll need to solve the Colossus Ruins puzzle.

3 To remember where you had him dig, you might want to go out and gather a number of bones and bring them back to Dog Fort, stockpile them by the fence, then go out and get more bones until you have at least fifteen. When you return, you'll have plenty of bones to experiment with, until you find all six gems.

4 Pluck a flea off yourself and give it to the Captain. If you don't have any fleas, return to the Dog Fort for a brief visit, then return to Pirate Beach and give the Captain a flea. (Every trip to Dog Fort gives you fleas—the longer you hang around there, the more fleas you'll wind up with. Gross!) While you're in the ship's cargo hold, have a look around—you can see some strange things down here!

5 Have you checked yourself for fleas? You'll pick them up invisibly whenever you enter the Dog Fort area. Too many of them and you'll scratch yourself to death. You can always try passing them on to someone else, you know, such as the Captain.

6 Make sure your Moodmeter is set to Lying when you visit Fluffy, and he'll give you a Leather Mouse. The Leather Mouse is used to identify the elemental associations in the Hieroglyphics Room and for raising the sphere statues that surround the Colossus Ruins statue.

7 The six gems. See "Dog Fort" for more information on uncovering the six gems. As you place each gem on the Altar, you'll find out each one's elemental property. The properties are Ruby = Fire, Sapphire = Lightning, Diamond = Moon, Emerald = Wind, Topaz = Sun, and Amethyst = Rain.

8 Jungle 2, which is one screen right of Dog Fort. Clear the bushes in the lower right corner of Jungle 2 and you'll uncover a hole in the ground. You only need to clear the bushes once to lighten the Ruins Room.

9 The Leather Mouse, which Fluffy will give you if you "Lie" to him and tell him that you are sympathetic to his Revolution.

10 Click the Leather Mouse on each hieroglyphic to see which gem it represents. They are, from left to right: Moon, Sun, Rain, Wind, Lightning, Fire.

11 Click the Leather mouse on one of the spheres to raise them all to their original shapes.

12 The solution to this puzzle—which gem goes with which statue—is easy to figure out once you've gathered the six clues from the Altar of Cats and the six clues from the Hieroglyphics Room. The correct order is Ruby, Sapphire, Emerald, Amethyst, Topaz, Diamond.

13 Be careful with it, for it will turn anything you touch with it into a mouse! If you turn yourself into a mouse by accident, go see Fluffy, who will give you some cheese to turn yourself back into Malcolm again.

14 Thanks to your actions, the enslaved Cats are now free. Fluffy is most grateful. And he's still helpful to you, should you accidentally turn the Crystal Mouse magic on yourself. Come visit him and he'll give you some cheese, which, when you eat it, will restore you to your Malcolmy self.

15 Louie, the peg-leg pirate.

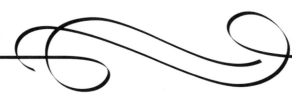

CHAPTER 15

THE ENDS OF THE EARTH

Double-crossed! That dirty, flea-bitten, no-good Jean Claude lied to you and dumped you right into the hands of Herman, Kallak, and Brandon. On their orders, the Pirate Captain dumps you a second time here at the Ends of the Earth! Except for three coins (back-wages from the work you did for Rowena in prison), you're empty-handed and practically all washed up. But all is not completely lost, sicko jester. By making three purchases and using those items wisely, you

Castle Gate

can get off this soaking wet stack of rock and water and make your way back to Kyrandia.

The Ends of the Earth

MISSION OBJECTIVE

Your objective is to figure out a way to navigate the falls successfully, visiting the Three Caves of Wonder along the way.

This chapter is more of a puzzle than a quest. Unlike the other chapters, you won't get any "Second Chances" here if you die. So, to give you a fair chance of escaping the Ends of the Earth on your own, let's break from the program a little and look at what you have to work with. If, after some back-breaking experimentation, you're sick and tired of falling to your death, feel free to skip ahead to "Enough Already—Get Me Outta Here," for the quickest way out.

GENERAL TIPS

Read these tips carefully to figure out how to use the items you can purchase to flee the Ends of the Earth alive.

THE VENDING MACHINES

The vending machines are here to help you. There are a total of five things for sale. However, you only have three coins, so you must make your purchases wisely.

The vending machine on the left distributes insurance policies. Buying one is a good idea—don't forget to take it with you when you leave this first screen, or else the policy is null if you die. Having the insurance policy on hand, in the event of your untimely death, you will return to the top of the falls, with two coins for buying different equipment and trying again.

The vending machine on the right distributes four kinds of equipment: swim fins, cleats, an umbrella, and a pool toy. Click the red buttons to change selections. Each item comes with its own "removal" item, with which you can remove the item once you wear it. Each removal item has its own, secondary use.

The equipment's "removal" items and "removal" item uses are described here:

Cleats: Shoehorn, which can be used to jimmy one additional item from the machine

Swim fins: Bungee cord, which acts as a tightrope bridge between two barely visible hooks in one scene

Pool toy: Pump, which can puff up a puffball flower. When jumped on, the puffball flower works like a trampoline in one scene to bounce you from one side of the waterfall to the other

Umbrella: Case, which is in and of itself useless, but when you put the umbrella in its case it can be used to swing you across the waterfall in one scene

THE THREE CAVES OF WONDER

Your goal at the Ends of the Earth is to visit the Three Caves of Wonder. Enter all three mysterious caves, and you will get out of here. You will always enter Cave 1 first, no matter which waterfall level you're on when you find your first cave.

With these two bits of information (and the two bits you've got left over to buy equipment), perhaps you'll have a better chance of leaving here alive. If not, you can always say . . .

ENOUGH ALREADY— GET ME OUTTA HERE!

Let's cut to the chase: At the top of the falls, buy the pool toy, and the umbrella.

Put on the pool toy, then jump into the waterfall (be careful not to click on the rocks!).

You'll land safely on the cliff with the "No Pool Toys" sign. (Don't remove the pool toy just yet.) Use the pump (the pool toy "removal" tool) in your inventory to inflate the puffball plant growing here by clicking on it a few times.

On the other side, enter the first Cave of Wonder.

After you exit the first cave, wear the pool toy again, if you aren't already. Never mind what the sign says—go ahead and jump into the waterfall wearing the pool toy.

You'll land safely on the cliff across from the "No Umbrellas" and "No Swim Fins" signs.

Remove the pool toy with the pump "removal" tool.

Click the closed umbrella on the hook sticking out from the middle of the falls.

Once you're on the left side, click the umbrella on yourself, then click on the cliff below you to descend. (Don't click on the waterfall!)

You'll land safely on the cliff bearing two signs: "No Cleats," and "No Umbrellas."

Enter the second Cave of Wonder on your left.

When you exit the second Cave of Wonder, make sure you're still holding your umbrella.

Like the last leap, click on the cliffs below you to float down to the next landing.

You'll land safely on a cliff bearing a "No Swim Fins" sign. You made it! The worst is over (. . . at least where the falls are concerned).

Now, enter the third Cave of Wonder on your left, and proceed to the next chapter.

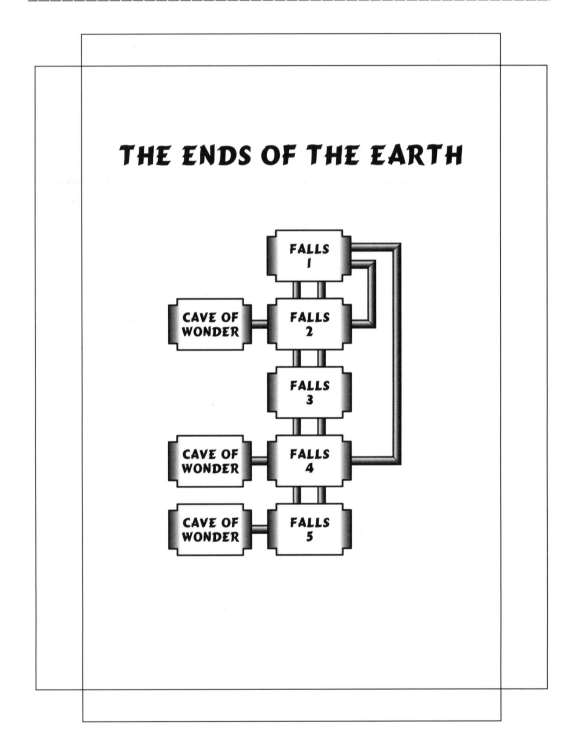

CHAPTER 16

FISH WORLD AND THE UNDERWORLD

Okay, so maybe this place you've wound up in seems worse than death by waterfall. It is pretty frightening here, what with that Fish Queen belting out orders, and those scantily-clad Mermen scooting to and fro. Sorry, pal, but if you knew that this was where you'd end up after the Three Caves of Wonder, you might have decided to cash in your chips once and for all.

Welcome to Limbo. Meet the Queen. Something else, isn't she? What, we're not sure. Bad news: She's the boss here and you'll have

The Fish Court

to play by her rules, unless you can figure a way out of here, of course.

MISSION OBJECTIVE

Your objective is to leave Limbo, via the Underworld, and get back to Kyrandia to clear you name, once and for all! You can find your way to the Underworld easily enough; however the Queen will repeatedly summon you back before you can make your escape. It's this obstacle—disabling the Queen's summoning power—that you'll need to overcome to move forward.

TIC-TAC-TOE FROM HELL

Every time you start to make sense of this place, the Queen will summon you to the Royal Chamber for a game of Tic-Tac-Toe. As long as you win, she'll want to keep playing.

Perhaps letting *her* win would be a more tactful strategy.[1] And flattery, as they say, will get you everywhere.[2]

Hint: There is a way to avoid playing the Queen's game, by bribing the Queen's right-hand (or is that, fin?) Merman.[3]

ED'S DISCOUNT UNDERWORLD EXPRESS

Yes, indeed, this horny little fish is your ticket out of Limbo and to the Underworld Entrance. It costs five coins to get blasted out or ten coins if you're blasted and wind up returning here for another try (because the Queen has summoned you back before you were able to leave the Underworld).

Fish World

To get coins, you'll have to visit Buddy at the Garbage Dump. He'll buy trash items from you. To get there quickly, ride the garbage sluice, in the upper left corner. The sluice will dump you right in the middle of the dump, where, if you click around a little, you'll find some trashy items you can sell to the Buddy the Blind bat-fish.[4]

Money Saving Hint: There is a way to reach the Underworld entrance without having to pay Ed any coins. It involves damaging the sluice, but not in this scene with Ed—elsewhere, in a scene of towering proportions.[5]

Fish World

BUDDY'S GARBAGE DUMP

The little creature hanging upside down in the cave is Buddy the Bat-fish. True to his name, he's as blind as a bat. He'll trade you coins for things that you bring him. Because he's blind, he'll believe that almost anything you bring him is valuable. While you'll find stuff lying around Fish World, there isn't much to pick up.

The Fish World Dump

The trash pile here is ripe with items, however you can't get to it from Limbo. You'll have to visit Ed's Underworld Express and ride the sluice, which will take you to the trash pile. Once you land in it, you can pick up two or three items before Buddy chases you off.

Another way to collect items to sell to Buddy is by raiding his little cave. He's guarding it, so you'll have to distract him with something. Actually, almost anything will work, providing you place it close enough for him to smell. The smell will lure him away momentarily, making it easy for you to take items out of his cave.[6]

By engaging Buddy in conversation while your Moodmeter is set to Lying, he'll think you're the tax man and will hand over two coins for back taxes.[7]

THE FISH TOWER

This is where you'll start when you first arrive in Fish World. There may be items here, a gold key even. Take anything you find. The only use for these items is selling them to Buddy the Bat-fish, at the Garbage Dump.

Worm taken.

Notice how the Fish Tower supports the overhead sluice? Perhaps if you were able to coax the fish holding up the sluice into shifting position, you could reorient the sluice's path.[8] Hint: The fish have an appetite for worms. To uncover one of these, you'll have to do a little munching yourself.[9]

PERCH UNIVERSITY

What a boring class! The only useful thing here is that apple sitting on the professor's desk. To get it, you'll have to cause a distraction.

Hint: Weren't you the class clown in your younger years? What a *laugh*![10]

Perch University

If you take the apple, another one will appear here when you leave and come back. You can sell the apple to Buddy at the Garbage Dump or eat it yourself.[11]

THE UNDERWORLD ENTRANCE

To reach the Underworld Entrance, you'll have to either pay Ed for a ride[12] or reconfigure the sluice somehow so that it sends you to the Underworld Entrance rather than to Buddy's Garbage Dump.[13]

Before you can walk through the Underworld Entrance, however, the Queen will summon you back for yet another game of Tic Tac Toe. The only way to get out of here is by putting an end to the Queen's power over you. No, filleting her won't do. You'll have to be more creative than that.

Have you talked to the woman at the desk at the Underworld Entrance? When you ask her about Missing Persons, she'll tell you that King Yrgmumph is missing, and that the only way to bring him back is by conducting a Royal Séance.

Gold coin taken.

After you conduct a Royal Séance, the Queen can no longer summon you back for Tic Tac Toe games.

To walk through the Underworld Entrance you'll have to get to the head of the line. You can try being nice to the farmer, and he may let you cut ahead. Or you can try distracting him by dropping something of value on the floor nearby.[14]

THE ROYAL SÉANCE

The Underworld Entrance clerk will tell you exactly which items you'll need for conducting a Royal Séance: "Something that looks back in time,"[15] "A likeness of the individual,"[16] and, "The presence of at least seven mortals who wish for the departed monarch to return."[17]

Put the first item on the ground beside the Queen, and after seven mortals are present, click second item on the first item to create the Royal Séance.

Hint: Once the King reclaims his place on the throne, boogie out of there fast—he's not a pleasant man to talk to.

THE UNDERWORLD LOBBY

Welcome to Underworld! What an exclusive club this is! They won't let just anyone stay here, so they'll have to process your application to see if you're up to their low, low standards.

The kind clerk here informs you that she has ordered your files from Kyrandia but is having trouble getting through. While you're waiting for an answer, you'll meet a few oddball characters. Just when you think you're going to like living here, the now-nervous clerk returns with bad news: There's been an error with your paperwork, and it looks like you'll have to return to the surface.

She'll direct you to the transport tube and then jet you to the Boondocks—a way-station of sorts, in the middle of the Earth. 'Fraid

The Lobby

your only choice here is to get on the auger machine and pedal your butt back to the surface. Oh well, it was fun while it lasted.

Tremendous Disappointment Points: 247

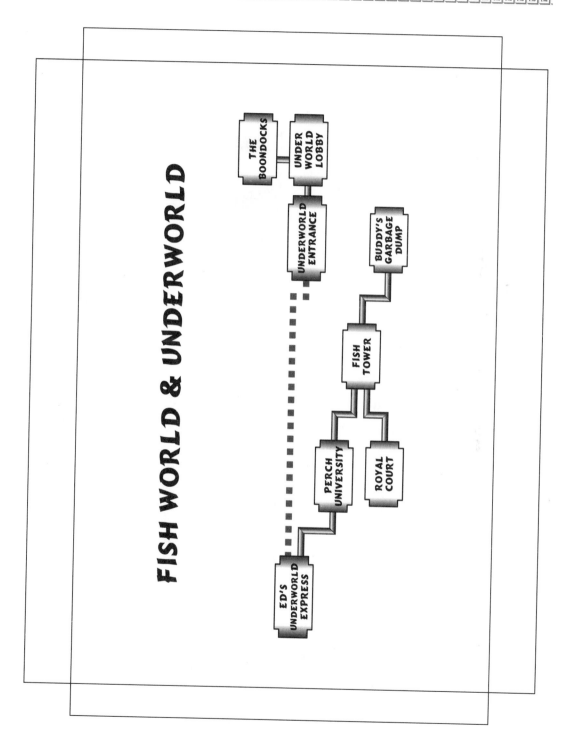

FISH WORLD & UNDERWORLD

THE BOONDOCKS

UNDER WORLD LOBBY

UNDERWORLD ENTRANCE

BUDDY'S GARBAGE DUMP

FISH TOWER

PERCH UNIVERSITY

ROYAL COURT

ED'S UNDERWORLD EXPRESS

CLUENOTES

[1] Let her win and she'll let you leave—for a while, anyway.

[2] Which is to say, make sure your Moodmeter is set to Lying when you're in the Queen's presence so that you can flatter her silly.

[3] Give him a coin before you make your first Tic-Tac-Toe move, and he'll take over for you, letting you slip out of the Queen's chamber. To get coins, you'll need to visit the Garbage Dump and Buddy, the Blind Bat-fish.

[4] Usually, you can collect two or three garbage items before Buddy will kick you out.

[5] Have you visited the Fish Tower, yet?

[6] Place an item in the space to Buddy's right and he'll leave his cave to check it out. While he's clear of the cave, snatch the two or three items from inside and then sell them back to him.

[7] You can leave and return and repeat this trick again and again.

[8] By feeding the bottom fish two worms, it will swell big and fat and cause the sluice to rupture, changing it's trajectory. Next time you ride the sluice, you'll be launched to the Underworld Entrance instead of the Dump.

[9] Have you found an apple? By eating it twice, you'll come up with a wriggling worm. An apple can be found at the Perch University and sometimes in Buddy's Garbage Dump cave.

[10] Tickle the student perch fish on the left with your Jester's Staff.

[11] Two bites on the apple will reveal a worm. The bottom fish at the Fish Tower loves worms. Feeding him two worms will have a pleasantly destructive effect on the sluice above.

[12] See "Buddy's Garbage Dump" for info on how to get money to pay for Ed's service.

13 Feed two worms to the bottom fish at the Fish Tower and he'll bloat up so fat that he'll damage the sluice, above. Next time you ride the sluice over at Ed's Underworld Express, you'll land at the Underworld Entrance, rather than in the Dump.

14 Drop a coin on the floor, and he'll leave his place in line to pick it up.

15 An old newspaper, which you can usually get at Buddy's Garbage Dump after a few tries at distracting the blind Bat-fish away from his cave entrance. See "Buddy's Garbage Dump" for more info on how to distract Buddy.

16 Have you looked closely at the coins down here? Indeed, that certainly is the Fish King!

17 Let's see, while playing Tic-Tac-Toe, there's you and the Queen's right-hand Merman, which makes two. Playing the game until five Mermen are on the board makes a total of seven mortals. With seven present, place the newspaper on the ground in the Royal Chamber, then click the coin on the newspaper to conduct a Royal Séance.

CHAPTER 17

BACK TO KYRANDIA

Finally, you're back to Kyrandia! But what's this? The machine you drove up from the middle of the earth has knocked a huge rock here aside, freeing Stewart, your good conscience, who has been trapped beneath the rock for so many years. Gunther, for one, is none too happy about this little reunion. Neither are you. Looks like you're going to have to choose between Good, Evil, or Both. What do you mean you can't decide? Wha'? Me? You want *me* to decide? But . . .

what if I choose the wrong side?[1] Okay, okay, I'll pick. Eeenie, meenie, minee, moe . . . .

MISSION OBJECTIVE

Your goal in this final chapter is to prove yourself innocent of the murders of King William and Queen Katherine. Eventually, anyway. First, you're going to have to rid Kyrandia of those pesky (and smelly) Pirates. After that, you'll need to arrange your own Trial at the Town Hall and conduct a Royal Séance with King William to finally reveal what *really* went down the night of the murders!

TROUBLE IN PARADISE

Though it's nighttime in Kyrandia, you can plainly see that things don't look quite right. After some wandering around, you'll eventually be captured and taken to the Castle Foyer.

Visit the Castle Dump first to recover some of your lost items.

Indeed, Captain Jean Claude—the self-appointed King of Kyrandia—has used the Crystal Mouse spell on the populace and taken control of your former stomping grounds. Brandon and Kallak are here too, both looking rather mousy.

Jean Claude is too stuck on himself to even acknowledge you. Hint: He won't talk to you or accept gifts until after you return from the Isle of Cats.

After a brief chat, Louie the pirate may turn you into a mouse as well,[2] and send you off to the Temporary Jail.

THE TEMPORARY JAIL

What was once Zanthia's Magician's Lodge has been turned into the Temporary Jail, where you'll be tossed if Louie the pirate turns you into a mouse. As a mouse, you'll encounter Duane, Zanthia, and Vince here as well.

(If you're not turned into a mouse, you should still come here, unlock the door, and free the trio locked up here.[3])

The Temporary Jail

Now, how to escape? Did you happen to get a nail at the Castle Dump before Louie apprehended you? If not, you can get one here, but only after causing a laugh riot of sorts.[4] Use the nail on the chains around your ankle to free yourself,[5] then you can free the others here as well, if you like.[6]

Now that you're free (and your fellow inmates as well), you've got to bust out of the Jail. Did you get the three items here?[7] Just the right ingredients to make a Sesame Seed bomb![8] You're free!

Once you're free, Zanthia will feed you a piece of cheese that will turn you back to your clowny self.

Downtown Kyrandia

THE PIRATES AND THE CAT JEWELS

If you didn't hear about it the first time around, on a second visit to the Castle Foyer you learn of the Pirates' desire to trade six large jewels for the return of your beloved homeland. Six large jewels can only mean, of course, a return to the Isle of Cats, where you found six jewels on your previous stay.

LEAVING KYRANDIA AGAIN

To get to the Isle of Cats, you'll need either Zanthia's Pegasus Potion, or Brandywine's Portal Potion. Do you remember how to obtain these? Which one to use depends on whether you chose a good conscience, a bad conscience, or both.[9]

To use the Portal Potion, take it to the Town Square, stand on the two footprints, then drink the potion.

To use the Pegasus Potion, take it to the Pegasus Landing, stand in the center of the circle, then drink the potion.

Pegasus potion taken.

TOWN HALL

To get here, you'll need to drop down the hole in the floor in the Toy Factory to reach the Cellar, then climb up the Cellar steps to reach the Town Hall.

Important Note: To exit the Town Hall, you must return to the Cellar, then climb up the sewer spout, which will return you to the Toy Factory.

Empty flask taken.

Inside the Town Hall, Zanthia will be working on her potion. (Assuming, that is, you freed her from the Temporary Jail.) Like the first time around, she needs Essence of Horse[10] to complete the mixture for Pegasus Potion.

Bring her back a substitute for Essence of Horse, put it in the cauldron, and you'll have a Pegasus Potion. Drink it while standing in the center of the Pegasus Landing and you'll return to the Isle of Cats.

THE ISLE OF CATS: RE-DO

As soon as you arrive on the Isle of Cats, you'll need to pick up the machete from the (former) Pirate Beach so you can hack your way through the jungle and kill any snakes you encounter.

Once you've got the machete, you're first order of business is finding Fluffy. He's hiding out in the same place you met him the first time, to the right of the Altar of Cats.

Fluffy will tell you about his latest revolution. When you ask him if you can get some gems, he'll give you a cheesemaker, with which you can destroy the Cat Colossus. (Depending on which conscience you chose at the beginning of the chapter,[11] Fluffy may ask you to bring him ten dog bones before he'll give you a cheesemaker.)

Mysterious Jungle

Click the cheesemaker on yourself to operate it. Then feed the chunk of cheese to the Cat Colossus Statue. The statue will crumble, releasing the six gems you need to trade with the pirates.[12]

Cool magic Points: 287

To leave the Isle of Cats and return to Kyrandia, visit Fluffy one last time. He'll give you a can of cat food. When you open it and take a whiff, it will send you on a heady trip back to Kyrandia.

SOCKING IT TO THE PIRATES

When you return to the Castle, the Pirates will be waiting for you. Jean Claude still won't speak to you—not until you offer him a gem. Don't bother giving him more than one gem—he's still a dirty liar and won't release the town as promised. Unless, that is, you can force him out of Kyrandia. Hint: In your inventory, you have an item obtained in Fish World that would make a "fitting" gift for the dastardly Jean Claude.[13]

Collar taken.

Once you've gotten rid of Jean Claude, the other pirates will flee! Now, what to do about Kallak and Brandon? Feel free to make them each a chunk of cheese to turn them back into men, if you like.

Of course they'll ask you to release them.[14] However Kallak warns that scaring off the Pirates doesn't absolve you of your heinous crimes.

HERMAN'S PAWN SHOP

In case you haven't been here yet, Herman has turned the Old Baths into a Pawn Shop. When you talk to him, Herman will have a number of items for sale. If the item he shows you isn't what you want, leave and come back in and he'll show you another item. (You can pay for items with jewels, if you have any left over from your return trip to the Isle of Cats.) Hint: Be careful here—one item Herman will offer is deadly if purchased.[15]

Amethyst taken.

Important tip: If you're trying to buy sesame seeds from Herman, you must sell him something first, and he'll pay you in sesame seeds, rather than money. Sounds cheap, but you'll need these to create Fish Cream Sandwiches for the climactic Trial ending. If you don't have the item he's interested in purchasing, leave, come back in, and ask again.

THE TRIAL

With the Pirates gone and Kallak and Brandon still locked up, go visit the Town Hall. Zanthia will be gone; however the Sculpture will inform you that in order to conduct your trial, you must assemble all of the Kyrandian citizens. He'll also ask to see the artifacts you plan to use to summon William's ghost so that he can testify.[16]

KING WILLIAM'S SÉANCE

Remember how you conducted the Royal Séance in the Fish World? The same thing applies here. You'll need a likeness of the person you are contacting—in this case a portrait of King William, which you can find somewhere in town, very close to "home"[17]—and an item from the past, which, if you inspect the Town Hall carefully, is already present.[18]

As for the seven mortals, the Sculpture will override the requirement just long enough to get a preview of King William's Séance.

When you show William's portrait to the Sculpture, he'll inform you that it will be useful, in the right place. It will do fine here—click the portrait on an item from the past.[19]

King William will appear and tell the Sculpture that you, Malcolm, did not murder him or his wife, Queen Katherine. He'll say that there is a curse on the enchanted Knife, and that any person of Royal Kyrandian blood who handles the knife will be stabbed to death.

Once you and the Town Hall sculpture have witnessed King William's preview appearance, you'll still need to draw a crowd.

Now, what was the most crowded place in all of Kyrandia? Why, the Fish Cream Parlour, of course!

THE FISH CREAM PARLOUR

Yikes, the Fish Cream Sandwich machine is broken! You'll have to help Duane, the Fish Cream Parlour attendant, repair it, or repair it yourself, to draw the crowd back to witness your final trial. If you freed Duane from jail earlier, he'll show up here after your return from the Isle of Cats.

Cheese taken.

If Duane is still a mouse, give him some cheese and he'll return to his normal self. Ask him if he's going to make Fish Cream Sandwiches, and he'll complain that the machine is broken. Then, leave the Fish Cream Parlour for awhile. When you return, he'll have fixed the machine. You'll need to bring him some eels, sesame seeds,[20] and cream.[21]

If Duane isn't at the Fish Cream Parlour when you return from the Isle of Cats, you'll have to fix the machine yourself. Basically, you just need to push the machine upright, but you'll need a crank-like item to do this. Have you visited Herman's Pawn Shop at the Old Bath House yet? He'll have the right item for the job, providing you've chased off the pirates.[22]

ASSEMBLING THE TOWNSFOLK

To assemble the Kyrandian Townsfolk for the trial, you'll need to start up the Fish Cream Sandwich Machine. Once you've brought back all of the ingredients for Fish Cream Sandwiches (cream, eel, and sesame seeds), put them in the machine's hopper, then press the button on the counter to make a Fish Cream Sandwich. Take the Fish Cream Sandwich, but don't eat it.[23]

With the Fish Cream Sandwich machine running, the people of Kyrandia will once again swarm into the Fish Cream Parlour (the perfect crowd for a trial, wouldn't you say?). They won't come in while you're here, though, so wander a few screens away, then come back.

The Fish Cream Parlour

Once everyone's crowded back into the Fish Cream Parlour, you're ready to conduct the Royal Séance and get on the with Trial. When you ask Duane if he'll tell everyone to romp over to the Town Hall, he says they won't go—they're too excited about their sandwiches. How, you're probably wondering, will you conduct the Trial unless the crowd comes with you to the Town Hall? Better go ask the Sculpture at Town Hall for a little advice. Remember, he craves this store's specialty, so don't leave the Fish Cream Parlour empty-handed.[24]

THE GREAT BIG FINALE

The Sculpture at Town Hall will ask you to show him the artifacts you plan to use to summon King William's ghost. When you show him the portrait of King William, which you found under your bed in your apartment, he'll tell you that it may be part of the solution, but where's the rest? He means the crowd, which must be at the Town Hall to make the Royal Séance spell work. Or maybe not. Have you offered him the Sculpture a Fish Cream Sandwich?

The Sculpture will transport you, himself, and Marko's Cabinet to the Fish Cream Parlour. Once you are all there, click William's portrait on Marko's Cabinet, and King William will appear. He's going to lay down some pretty heavy news for you and the townsfolk, so kick back, relax, and enjoy the dramatic endgame show, cousin—this time you're really free![25]

Malcolm's Apartment

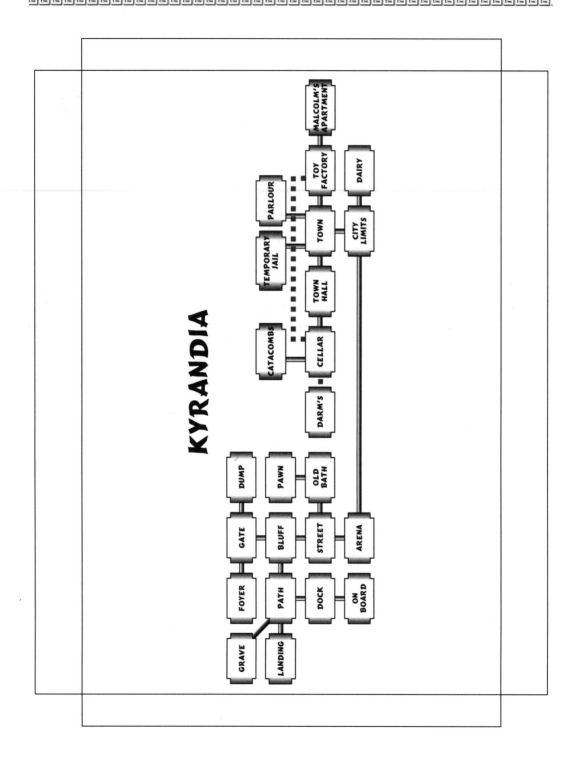

KYRANDIA

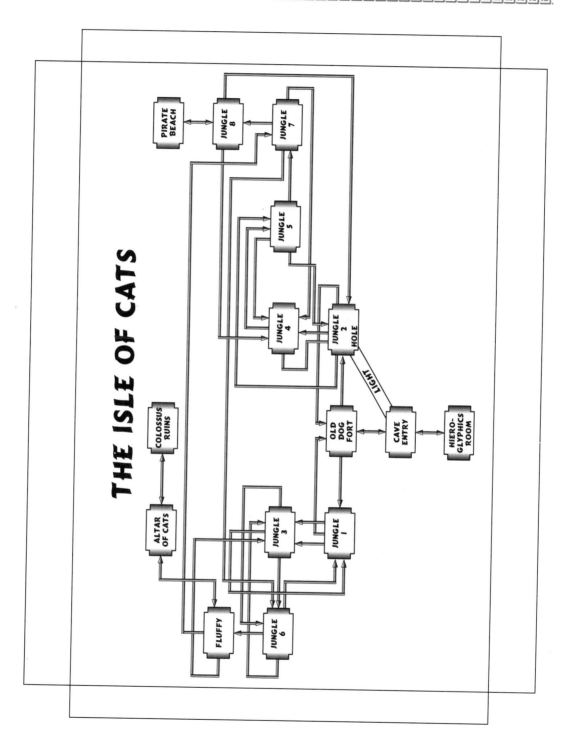

THE ISLE OF CATS

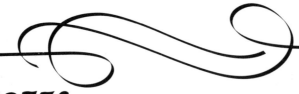

CLUENOTES

1 There is no "wrong" side. However, the conscience you choose, or both, will affect the rest of the game's humor and the situations that befall you. Also: From here on, your Moodmeter is no longer active. You could always choose one conscience, save your place, finish the game, then replay the game from this point again choosing the other conscience or both. Just for laughs, of course.

2 Only if you chose Stewart, your good conscience, at the beginning of the chapter.

3 Unless, that is, you chose Gunther at the beginning of this chapter. He wouldn't dream of letting you free these three!

4 Use your Jester's Staff a few times on the three locked up here, and they'll laugh so hard they'll pop a nail free from the wooden stockade.

5 You have to click the point of the nail on exactly the right place—the first link over from the cuff around your ankle.

6 It's a good idea, since you'll need the items they've got in order to knock down the jail door, and they will only offer them if they are freed.

7 A flask of water, an eel, and some sesame seeds.

8 First, fertilize the seeds by combining them with the eel. Next, place the fertilized seeds on the Jail door, then pour the flask of water on the seeds.

9 Brandywine will only trade you a Portal Potion for a squirrel if you are being guided by Gunther, your bad conscience—she won't believe that the "new" honest you, guided by Stewart, is real! So, if you are being guided by Stewart, or both, you'll have to use the Pegasus Potion to reach the Isle of Cats.

10 Drop a log of firewood (which you can get in front of the dairy) into the Toy Machine, flip the left lever on the machine up, and the lever on the right down, then press the green button. The machine will spit out a rocking horse, which you can give to Zanthia to create the potion.

Gunther or Stewart, Fluffy will give you the cheesemaker
lose both, Fluffy will ask you to bring him ten bones before
cheesemaker. You can find the bones scattered throughout the
behind bushes, or you can dig the bones up at the Old Dog Fort
machete as a shovel.

ly need to take one gem with you. However, you can take more to
y the purchase of items from Herman's Pawn Shop.

13 The Gold Collar, which came off your neck when you left Fish World. After
you hand out at least one gem to one of the pirates, Jean Claude will accept the
collar as a gift and will wear it. Tic-Tac-Toe, anyone?

14 Your nail won't work on their locks anyway, so go on outside and enjoy your
sweet revenge.

15 The Royal Enchanted Knife. Don't buy it!

16 In case you're confused about what's going on here, the Sculpture, now the
Town Judge, intends to conduct a trial, giving you the chance to clear you name.
Remember your trip to Katherine's Grave, at the beginning of the game? She
informed you that to reach King William you would need to conduct a Royal
Séance.

17 Like under your bed.

18 It was Marko's gift to Zanthia, the cabinet.

19 The magician's cabinet. Click William's portrait on the magician's cabinet to
call forth William's spirit.

20 Sell items to Herman and he'll pay you with Sesame Seeds.

21 For cream, you'll need to attract the cows home again at the dairy. Quick
reminder: You'll need to throw into the cow feed hopper two large sprouts,
which you can create by adding water to fertilized sesame seeds. Then the cows
will come back. Use a nail to puncture the cream container and collect some
cream in a flask. Bring the cream, a batch of plain sesame seeds, and an eel to
Duane and he'll whip up a Fish Cream Sandwich.

22 That little, "Y" shaped item he offers is actually the pirate Louie's crutch. Use this on the broken Fish Cream Sandwich Machine to prop it back into place.

23 Give it to the Sculpture in Town Hall, so that he changes the Royal Séance rules a little to accommodate your trial.

24 As a Fish Cream Sandwich is all you'll need now, then you're home free.

25 Say hello to your new life . . . Or is that wife? And Junior makes three!

MEET
THE KYRANDIA TEAM

Westwood Studios was founded by Brett W. Sperry and Louis Castle in 1985. The Westwood staff has produced entertainment software for the IBM PC, Amiga, and Macintosh, and in at least five foreign languages. Westwood is also a certified developer for the Nintendo, Super Nintendo, Sega, and NEC game systems. The growing CD ROM development division is currently the most active.

The company's success has been accomplished through amazing teamwork. As many as 80 employees now participate directly in product development. Programmers and designers coordinate their efforts with the company's sound, graphic art, and testing departments, and everybody seems to get involved in the last frantic months before a new product's release.

Critics and customers alike have praised many of Westwood's products, including the recent games: **The Legend of Kyrandia Books 1, 2 & 3**, **Lands of Lore**, and **Dune II**. Even the older titles like **BattleTech I & II**, **Hillsfar**, **DragonStrike**, and **Eye of the Beholder I & II** still inspire legions of dedicated fans.

It is really difficult to single out any individuals on the Westwood team, but 80 biographical blurbs seems a bit too much, so here's a sampling of personalities that were particularly active in creating the Kyrandia series:

BRETT SPERRY

* Started Westwood Studios, started the **Kyrandia**, **Eye of the Beholder**, and **Dune II** series, serves now as president/head visionary of Westwood.

* Equally at ease in a tuxedo or jeans.

* Adventurer, takes advantage of frequent opportunity to travel about Europe and the U.S. after conventions and trade shows. When home, likely to fill his car up with friends and head off for a weekend exploring ghost towns, or snorkeling through mountain streams.

RICK GUSH

* Hired to write dialog for **K1**, designed and produced **K2** and **K3**.
* Grumpy old wannabe playwright who is lucky enough to write better dialog than any of the programmers.
* Has had many different jobs, including rodeo work, uranium mining, sensuality counseling, and selling encyclopedias door to door in Mexico City.

MIKE LEGG

* Lead coder for all three **Kyrandia** games.
* Always the life of the party. Energy level is inspirational, works extremely hard 16 hours each day with little complaining.
* Tropical fish and a dazzlingly active social life. Wife Maria is also a Westwood programmer.

MIKE GRAYFORD

* Assistant coder for **K2** CD and **K3**.
* Match made in heaven. Extra smart, but disarmingly humble. Perfect companion and stabilizer for Mike Legg, and all the women in the office adore him.

DAVE POKORNY

* Managed production and dialog translations for **K3**.
* Mr. Details. MBA, produced cartridge versions of **Dune II** game, then joined **K3** to help Rick Gush manage project.

RICK PARKS

* Lead artist at Westwood.
* "Art God" has been producing the best computer art in the world for many years.
* Gigglebox, makes everyone feel like a wit.

JOE KUCAN

* Directed the vocal actors for **K2** and **K3**.
* Amusing personality punctures stereotype of arrogant theater types.
* Is now producing for Westwood, as well as continuing to head all video and vocal creation for multiple projects.

PAUL MUDRA

* Managed all sound technology for all three games.
* Technology whiz, keeps up with confusing world of sound technology.
* Very athletic, desert raised, avid hockey player and fan.

DWIGHT OKAHARA

* Did the sound effects for all three games.
* Another prankster, active musician.
* Techno-whiz.

FRANK KLEPACKI

* Wrote the music for all three games.
* Has written the music for all Westwood games in the last four years.
* Young punk, will be famous soon, possibly from his popular local heavy metal band.

**Programmers in playroom,
from front to back:**

Mike Grayford, Programmer;
Rick Gush, Writer and
Producer;
Maria Legg, Programmer;
Joe Kucan, Vocal Recording
Director;
Dwight Okahara
(hanging left), Audio design;
Dave Pokorny
(hanging right w/ glasses),
Assistant Producer;
Michael Legg (top center),
Lead Programmer.

**Artists in jungle background,
from left to right:**

TOP ROW: Shelly Johnson,
Jerry Moore, Jack Martin,
Ren Olsen, Chuck Carter
BOTTOM ROW: Ferby Miguel,
Cary Averett
BEING HELD IN CENTER:
Lenny Lee

COMPUTER GAME BOOKS

The 7th Guest: The Official Strategy Guide	$19.95
Aces Over Europe: The Official Strategy Guide	$19.95
Alone in the Dark: The Official Strategy Guide	$19.95
Betrayal at Krondor: The Official Strategy Guide	$19.95
CD-ROM Games Secrets, Volume 1	$19.95
Computer Adventure Game Secrets	$19.95
DOOM Battlebook	$14.95
DOOM II: The Official Strategy Guide	$19.95
Dracula Unleashed: The Official Strategy Guide & Novel	$19.95
Harpoon II: The Official Strategy Guide	$19.95
Lemmings: The Official Companion (with disk)	$24.95
Master of Orion: The Official Strategy Guide	$19.95
Microsoft Flight Simulator: The Official Strategy Guide	$19.95
Microsoft Space Simulator: The Official Strategy Guide	$19.95
Might and Magic Compendium: The Authorized Strategy Guide for Games I, II, III, and IV	$19.95 each
Myst: The Official Strategy Guide	$19.95
Outpost: The Official Strategy Guide	$19.95
Pagan: Ultima VIII—The Ultimate Strategy Guide	$19.95
Prince of Persia: The Official Strategy Guide	$19.95
Quest for Glory: The Authorized Strategy Guide	$19.95
Rebel Assault: The Official Insider's Guide	$19.95
Return to Zork Adventurer's Guide	$14.95
Secret of Mana Official Game Secrets	$14.95
Shadow of the Comet: The Official Strategy Guide	$19.95
Sherlock Holmes, Consulting Detective: The Unauthorized Strategy Guide	$19.95
Sid Meier's Civilization, or Rome on 640K a Day	$19.95
SimCity 2000: Power, Politics, and Planning	$19.95
SimEarth: The Official Strategy Guide	$19.95
SimFarm Almanac: The Official Guide to SimFarm	$19.95
SimLife: The Official Strategy Guide	$19.95
SSN-21 Seawolf: The Official Strategy Guide	$19.95
Strike Commander: The Official Strategy Guide and Flight School	$19.95
Stunt Island: The Official Strategy Guide	$19.95
SubWar 2050: The Official Strategy Guide (with disk)	$24.95
TIE Fighter: The Official Strategy Guide	$19.95
Ultima: The Avatar Adventures	$19.95
Ultima VII and Underworld: More Avatar Adventures	$19.95
Wing Commander I and II: The Ultimate Strategy Guide	$19.95
X-COM UFO Defense: The Official Strategy Guide	$19.95
X-Wing: The Official Strategy Guide	$19.95

VIDEO GAME BOOKS

Breath of Fire Authorized Game Secrets	$14.95
EA SPORTS Official Power Play Guide	$12.95
The Legend of Zelda: A Link to the Past—Game Secrets	$12.95
Maximum Carnage Official Game Secrets	$9.95
Mega Man X Official Game Secrets	$14.95
Mortal Kombat II Official Power Play Guide	$9.95
GamePro Presents: Nintendo Games Secrets Greatest Tips	$11.95
Nintendo Game Secrets, Volumes 1, 2, 3, and 4	$11.95 each
Parents's Guide to Video Games	$12.95
Sega CD Official Game Secrets	$12.95
GamePro Presents: Sega Genesis Games Secrets Greatest Tips, Second Edition	$12.95
Official Sega Genesis Power Tips Book, Volumes 2, and 3	$14.95 each
Sega Genesis Secrets, Volume 4	$12.95
Sega Genesis and Sega CD Secrets, Volume 5	$12.95
Sega Genesis Secrets, Volume 6	$12.95
Sonic 3 Official Play Guide	$12.95
Super Empire Strikes Back Official Game Secrets	$12.95
Super Mario World Game Secrets	$12.95
Super Metroid Unauthorized Game Secrets	$14.95
Super NES Games Secrets, Volumes 2, and 3	$11.95 each
Super NES Games Secrets, Volumes 4 and 5	$12.95 each
GamePro Presents: Super NES Games Secrets Greatest Tips	$11.95
Super NES Games Unauthorized Power Tips Guide, Volumes 1 and 2	$14.95 each
Super Star Wars Official Game Secrets	$12.95
TurboGrafx-16 and TurboExpress Secrets, Volume 1	$9.95
Urban Strike Official Power Play Guide, with Desert Strike & Jungle Strike	$12.95

TO ORDER BOOKS

Please send me the following items:

Quantity#	Title	Unit Price	Total
_____	_____	$_____	$_____
_____	_____	$_____	$_____
_____	_____	$_____	$_____
_____	_____	$_____	$_____
_____	_____	$_____	$_____
_____	_____	$_____	$_____
		Subtotal	$_____
		7.25% Sales Tax (California only)	$_____
		Shipping and Handling*	$_____
		Total Order	$_____

*$4.00 shipping and handling charge for the first book and $0.50 for each additional book.

BY TELEPHONE: with Visa or MC, call (916) 632-4400 Mon.–Fri., 9–4 PST
BY MAIL: just fill out the information below and send with your remittance to:

Prima Publishing
P.O. Box 1260BK
Rocklin, CA 95677

Satisfaction unconditionally guaranteed

My name is _____

I live at _____

City _____ State ____ Zip _____

MC/Visa # _____ Exp. _____

Signature _____

KYRANDIA BOOK I: THE LEGEND OF KYRANDIA

Called "one of the best adventure games" by Computer Game Review, the critically acclaimed first chapter of the Fables & Fiends series is available in both floppy and a gorgeously enhanced CD version. Intrigue abounds as you cast spells, search strangely lit caverns and chase down the murderous jester Malcolm. *Kyrandia* features brilliantly stunning graphics, synchronized speech for the CD version, and an extremely user-friendly interface.

KYRANDIA BOOK 2: THE HAND OF FATE

Now you see it, now you don't. The land of Kyrandia is disappearing piece by piece and you are the offbeat young mystic who must find a way to save it. Your surreal journey will twist even the sharpest of minds. Featuring breakthrough *Trulight* technology for cinematically illuminated scenery and a revolutionary *State-of-Mind* gameplay system, *The Hand Of Fate* is even more intricate and spellbinding than it's predecessor *The Legend Of Kyrandia*. Grasp *The Hand Of Fate* and kiss conventional logic goodbye.

KYRANDIA BOOK 3: MALCOLM'S REVENGE

In Book Three of the *The Legend Of Kyrandia*, you become Malcolm—the infamous Court Jester of Kyrandia. And you have one last chance to save your rude, misunderstood hide. Go to the ends of the earth armed with swimfins and an inflatable pool toy as you attempt to solve the murders behind the mad monarchy. But be careful, because your country despises you. The Underworld entices you. And pirates double-cross you. It's a fantasy world filled with magic—and the trick is to stay alive.

Visit your favorite computer store, or call (800) 874-4607 to order these or other Westwood Studios titles.

U.S. $19.95
Can. $27.95
U.K. £ 18.49 Net

Stop Clowning Around in Kyrandia...

REVENGE IS A DISH BEST SERVED HOT!

Just as lightning never strikes twice in the same place, you have but one chance to carry out Malcolm's twisted plan of revenge. Freed from the prison of stone in Book 3, you'll take Malcolm to The Isle of Cats, The Ends of the Earth, Fish World and The Underworld, and back to Kyrandia to create chaos. You'll need more than the magical toys in his black bag of tricks to complete this devious plot. You must have *The Legend of Kyrandia—The Official Strategy Guide*.

LOOK INSIDE FOR:

- Subtle clues that nudge you along the game-winning paths
- Easy-to-find hints and strategies for all three Kyrandia adventures
- Game-breaking puzzle solutions and answers
- Maps that completely annotate all three games
- And much more

COVERS ALL KYRANDIA GAMES FOR THE PC AND MACINTOSH

Joe Hutsko has authored numerous books for Prima, including _____ _____ ____ *The Official Insider's Guide* and *Pagan: Ultima VIII—The Ultimate Strategy Guide*. As a full-time writer, _____ digital fun have appeared in *GamePro*, *Multimedia World*, *PC Games*, *Electronic En_____* publications. He is a former technology advisor for Apple Computer, Inc.

PRIMA'S
SECRETS
OF THE GAMES

Secrets of the Games
An Imprint of Prima Publishing
Platform: CD-ROM

ISBN 1-55958-782-2

51995

EAN

9 781559 587822